The Cambridge Introduction to
Shakespeare's Poetry

Shakespeare's poems were enormously popular in his lifetime, but, aside from the enduring appeal of the Sonnets, are today much less familiar than his plays. This *Introduction* celebrates the achievement of Shakespeare as a poet, providing students with ways of understanding and enjoying his remarkable poems. It honors the aesthetic and intellectual complexity of the poems without making them seem unapproachably complicated, outlining their exquisite pleasures and absorbing enigmas. Schoenfeldt suggests that today's readers are better able to analyze aspects of the poems that were formerly ignored or the source of scandal – the articulation of a fervent same-sex love, for example, or the incipient racism inherent in a hierarchy of light and dark. By engaging closely with Shakespeare's major poems – *Venus and Adonis, Lucrece,* "The Phoenix and Turtle," and the Sonnets and *A Lover's Complaint –* the *Introduction* demonstrates how much these extraordinary poems still have to say to us.

MICHAEL SCHOENFELDT is Professor of English at the University of Michigan. He is the author of *Bodies and Selves in Early Modern England: Physiology and Inwardness in Spenser, Shakespeare, Herbert, and Milton* and *Prayer and Power: George Herbert and Renaissance Courtship,* and he has contributed to publications including *A Companion to Shakespeare's Sonnets* and *Imagining Death in Shakespeare and Milton.*

The Cambridge Introduction to
Shakespeare's Poetry

MICHAEL SCHOENFELDT

CAMBRIDGE
UNIVERSITY PRESS

CAMBRIDGE
UNIVERSITY PRESS

University Printing House, Cambridge CB2 8BS, United Kingdom

One Liberty Plaza, 20th Floor, New York, NY 10006, USA

477 Williamstown Road, Port Melbourne, VIC 3207, Australia

314-321, 3rd Floor, Plot 3, Splendor Forum, Jasola District Centre, New Delhi - 110025, India

79 Anson Road, #06-04/06, Singapore 079906

Cambridge University Press is part of the University of Cambridge.

It furthers the University's mission by disseminating knowledge in the pursuit of education, learning and research at the highest international levels of excellence.

www.cambridge.org
Information on this title: www.cambridge.org/9780521705073

© Michael Schoenfeldt 2010

First published 2010

A catalogue record for this publication is available from the British Library

Library of Congress Cataloging in Publication data
Schoenfeldt, Michael Carl.
The Cambridge introduction to Shakespeare's poetry / Michael Schoenfeldt.
    p.   cm. – (Cambridge introductions to literature)
Includes bibliographical references and index.
ISBN 978-0-521-87941-5 – ISBN 978-0-521-70507-3 (pbk.)
1. Shakespeare, William, 1564–1616 – Poetic works.   2. Narrative poetry,
English – History and criticism.   3. Shakespeare, William, 1564–1616. Sonnets.
4. Sonnets, English – History and criticism.   I. Title.
PR2984.S36   2010
821'.3 – dc22   2010029489

ISBN 978-0-521-87941-5 Hardback
ISBN 978-0-521-70507-3 Paperback

Contents

Acknowledgments

Because I have lived with this book for a long time, it demanded the patient cooperation of my closest relationships. I would like to thank Leslie Atzmon for indulging my obsession with Shakespeare's poetry, and for teaching me something about its ostensible subject of love. It is a pleasure to dedicate this book to her. I would like to thank as well Ben and Aaron, who have grown up tolerating their father's frequently tedious disquisitions on various early modern writers even as they reminded me that there were many other aspects of life that were well worth attending to.

Both Niels Herold and Valerie Traub took time from their own wonderful work on Shakespeare to apply critical pressure to the chapters on the Sonnets. Patrick Cheney read the entire manuscript with his characteristic rigor and unmatched generosity; his comments saved me from a hundred embarrassing mistakes in the process. Sarah Stanton was the kind of editor everyone hopes for, eminently patient and deeply intelligent even when gently prodding.

The remarkable early modern community at Michigan is an unremitting source of intellectual stimulation and emotional support. I would like to thank all the members of the English 450 class on the poetry of Shakespeare; their pointed questions and unique voices infuse this book. The graduate students at Michigan provide a remarkably vibrant and nurturing community punctuated by individual brilliance. Andrew Bozio deserves special notice for his painstaking work on the manuscript and index of this book, as well as for helping me think through several important issues of Shakespeare's poetry. It is a privilege to teach at a place that continues to attract such wonderful students.

Acknowledgements

Shakespeare and English poetry

> Anyone can be creative; it's rewriting other people that's a challenge.
> – Bertolt Brecht

Most students and some scholars are surprised to learn that Shakespeare's greatest publishing success in his lifetime was *Venus and Adonis*. They are also surprised to learn that Shakespeare at his death was at least as well known for his non-dramatic poetry as for his work in the theater. Attention to the non-dramatic poetry tends to get swamped by the interest inevitably generated by the remarkable and sustained accomplishment of the plays. This tendency to marginalize the non-dramatic verse is a process at least as old as the First Folio of 1623, in which the compilers, for whatever reason, fail to include *Venus and Adonis, Lucrece,* the Sonnets, and "The Phoenix and Turtle," in their collection of Shakespeare's works. Prior to the First Folio, though, the tendency was for publishers to advertise Shakespeare's accomplishments in non-dramatic poetry. William Jaggard, whose son Isaac published the First Folio, had in 1599 issued a work designed to capitalize on Shakespeare's growing fame as a poet: *The Passionate Pilgrim* (1599). A collection of twenty poems purported to be by Shakespeare, this volume prints several poems from an early comedy by Shakespeare, *Love's Labour's Lost,* as well as versions of two of the sonnets that would eventually be published in the 1609 Sonnets, and several poems by other poets. Many of the poems in *The Passionate Pilgrim* involve the theme of Venus and Adonis, repeatedly identified with Shakespeare since it was the subject of his biggest hit. Other poems in *The Passionate Pilgrim* deal with the myth of Philomel, one of the several narratives behind Shakespeare's popular *Lucrece.*[1] Aspiring to make money on Shakespeare's growing reputation as a poet, Jaggard had no doubts that Shakespeare was at once a poet and a playwright. Shakespeare, then, was not just a dramatist who happened to compose a few poems in his spare time; rather, he was, in Patrick Cheney's

1

useful term, a "poet-playwright." [2] Like a fine athlete who uses the same muscle group for different sports, Shakespeare moves with facility between the two intimately related pursuits of poetry and drama.

When reading Shakespeare's non-dramatic poems, it is nonetheless important to remember that Shakespeare was one of the great writers of comic and tragic drama, if only because this encourages us to look for related elements in the poems. Indeed, I hope that this *Introduction* will allow readers to see afresh the comedy embedded in the clumsy but lush eroticism of *Venus and Adonis*, as well as the tragedy stemming from the disturbing physical and psychological violence in *Lucrece*. It might also help us to comprehend the mysterious mathematics of human amatory relationships in "The Phoenix and Turtle," and the astonishing gamut of expressions of emotional commitment and erotic betrayal in the Sonnets. This *Cambridge Introduction* is designed to celebrate the achievement of Shakespeare's poems, to investigate what they have to say to us at this moment in cultural history, and to make available to today's reader some sense of the range and intelligence of current engagements with them. While poetry is certainly a central element of the plays, this volume focuses on Shakespeare's remarkable forays into non-dramatic poetry, in the effort to correct the imbalance of attention. While the Sonnets have been the subject of much scrutiny – some of it profoundly critical and scholarly, but much of it glorified rumor-mongering or biographical speculation – the other poems have been almost completely ignored outside the academy.

This is, finally, a book about magic – the magic that can lead a particular combination of words to produce pleasure and meaning in readers centuries later. Shakespeare in fact self-consciously aspires to perform this magic repeatedly in his Sonnets, and even makes this aspiration the theme of many of them. "Not marble nor the gilded monuments / Of princes shall outlive this pow'rful rhyme," brags the opening of Sonnet 55. The speaker of that poem outrageously claims that his poetry is more powerful and perdurable than the most apparently immutable monuments – a claim that is validated every time the poems are read (and would cease to have truth value when they are no longer read). This is the miraculous transformation celebrated in Shakespeare's Sonnet 65 – "That in black ink my love may still shine bright." "Still" here means both "always" and "yet"; Shakespeare here asserts that something as ephemeral as love can be rendered perpetual through art. He asks the transient media of ink and paper to perform a kind of transubstantiation on the fleeting desires experienced by transient beings toward transient beings, converting impermanence to infinity. As Shakespeare claims in the concluding couplet of Sonnet 18, "So long as men can breathe or eyes can see, / So long lives this, and this gives life to thee."

As I write this, the volume *Shakespeare's Sonnets* celebrates its 400 birthday; men (and women) are still breathing, eyes are still seeing, and the literary accomplishment of these phenomenal poems still shines remarkably bright. One testament to the continuing resonance of Shakespeare's remarkable literary accomplishments occurred recently. On April 23, 2009, in honor of the 445th anniversary of Shakespeare's birth, the city of Chicago, Illinois, declared, via mayoral proclamation, the day to be "Talk Like Shakespeare Day" in Chicago. Posters were produced with such advice as "Instead of *you*, say *thou*. Instead of *y'all*, say *thee*." And "Instead of cursing, try calling your tormenters jack-anapes or canker-blossoms or poisonous bunch-back'd toads." The poster also recommends:

> When in doubt, add the letters "eth" to the end of verbs (he runneth, he trippeth, he falleth). To add weight to your opinions, try starting them with methinks, mayhaps, in sooth or wherefore.

"Talk Like Shakespeare Day" offers good-humored testimony to the remark-able cultural clout that Shakespeare continues to wield. It is a statement of the abiding relevance of Shakespeare, and the effort, via genial fun, to commemo-rate the near miracle by which a Stratford commoner became the most revered poet in the English language.

But the defining rubric of the civic commemoration also suggests that Shakespeare speaks a language significantly different from our own; it indicates that only through a deliberate effort can we speak, or comprehend, the language of Shakespeare. The purpose of this volume is not to help one learn to speak like Shakespeare; rather, it is to help today's reader understand the rich and varied ways that Shakespeare's poetic language works. The commentary will be designed to provide readers with ways of understanding, appreciating, and enjoying these emotionally intense and highly wrought poems. I intend to honor the aesthetic and intellectual complexity of these poems without making them seem impossibly, and unapproachably, complicated. In order to do this, I will bring in large contextual issues when this is necessary to the understanding of a poem, but will for the most part focus on the close reading of individual stanzas and poems.

It is important to remember that even experienced readers sometimes need help with Shakespeare's language and syntax. Those of us who have dedicated significant portions of our lives to Shakespeare still find that his words can prove difficult to comprehend; indeed, sometimes they get harder rather than easier to understand with study. This is partly because Shakespeare sometimes uses words no longer current in English. It is also a function of the fact that he uses words that are themselves familiar, but whose meanings have changed over time. At the end of *A Lover's Complaint*, for example, the injured maid complains of her former lover that "When he most burnt in heart-wished luxury, / He preached pure maid, and praised cold chastity" (lines 314–15). Although it might seem to a contemporary reader that the maid is blaming her lover for his expensive taste, she is actually castigating him for his hypocritical lust. "Luxury" was a word closely linked to lechery in the early modern lexicon – a point which a modern reader can easily miss.

At the same time, vestiges of Shakespeare's language and images linger in our vocabulary, even when we are not aware of them. Shakespeare's works have so completely permeated our language that certain plays can seem almost too familiar, even on a first reading. I had a student several years ago who told me that he would like *Hamlet* better if it did not include so many clichés. The student was not wrong, however naive the comment. *Hamlet* has been so fully absorbed into the culture that it is sometimes hard to hear it afresh, even for first-time readers or spectators. Phrases such as "in my mind's eye," "to thine own self be true," or "Though this be madness, yet there is method in it," can sound stale to the twenty-first-century reader simply because of the play's immense and continuing impact on our culture.

For better and worse, this is less of a problem with Shakespeare's poems. Certain sonnets have been comfortably absorbed into the lexicon – Sonnet 18 ("Shall I compare thee to a summer's day?"), for example, has become proverbial for expressions of tender affection, and Sonnet 116 ("Let me not to the marriage of true minds") is frequently heard in various commitment ceremonies (in part because it articulates a marriage of ungendered minds, not gendered bodies). But, in general, Shakespeare's poetry is far less well known than his most popular plays; perhaps our comparative ignorance of the poems can be an asset, allowing us to hear them with fresh ears.

Versification and meter

When reading Shakespeare's poetry, it is important to remember that experiences and emotions are raw, messy things that rarely resolve themselves into fourteen lines of metrically regular rhymed verse without some effort. Shakespeare's contemporaries understood that effort, and praised him for his smooth lyric surface. There is in fact a kind of gratifying regularity in the standard Shakespearean line, which makes the deviations from this norm all the more effective. A kind of music emerges from the blend of expectation and surprise, and this music can provide a key to the meaning and mood of the lines, if we have ears to hear.

Form is never just the container of emotion, however; rather, affect is also a function of form. Certain forms, in other words, express, and even produce, certain affects. Any single poem, moreover, is the combination of a nearly infinite possible combination of words. When reading Shakespeare's poetry, it is particularly important to pay attention to the formal and linguistic qualities of his poetry. The aural and rhythmic qualities of words cluster to produce subliminal and somatic effects that underpin or subvert the overt semantic sense; these are the fundamental building blocks of Shakespeare's poetic art. Shakespeare loves to explore the ambiguities lurking in the polyglot language that was Elizabethan English. Reading his poetry with an *Oxford English Dictionary* (*OED*) at hand is always rewarding, because of his remarkable ability to exploit the etymological roots, the secondary and tertiary meanings, and even false etymologies, of the words he uses. When the speaker of Sonnet 92, for example, declares that "I see a better state to me belongs / Than that which on thy humor doth depend" (lines 7–8), the contemporary reader can be confused or even misled if operating under the assumption that the current meaning of "humor" as "the tendency to provoke laughter" is operative. But a quick glance at the *OED* reveals that "humor" has a rich and complex history; deriving originally from the four humoral fluids thought to cause various emotional states, the word comes to mean the whims or moods elicited by these fluids.[3] The speaker of Sonnet 92, in other words, argues he deserves better treatment than his capricious audience currently provides.

Reading the poetry out loud is always useful as well. This is in part because complex syntactic patterns – with inversions of standard word order for purposes of meter and rhyme – frequently reveal their grammatical structure when enunciated. But it is also important to read the poetry out loud because only then can the music or cacophony of a given line be fully apprehended. Shakespeare's characteristic verse line is iambic pentameter, ten syllables with every second one stressed. In the plays, the pentameter is largely non-rhyming, which is rather curiously called "blank verse." Hamlet even jokes with Rosencrantz about metrics when a troop of players visit Denmark, suggesting that "The lady shall say her mind freely – or the blank verse shall halt for't" (*Hamlet*, 2.2.302–03). Shakespeare's verse is unusually flexible, allowing a wide range of rhythmical effects. It should not be understood as a set of strict rules but as a flexible array of practices rooted in dramatic necessity.

Even as the plays use poetry, they also imagine characters who abuse poetry. *The Two Gentlemen of Verona* at once mocks the use of "wailful sonnets" in courtship, and explores "the force of heaven-bred poesy" (3.2.69, 71). Theseus in *A Midsummer Night's Dream* famously links "the lunatic, the lover, and the poet" as figures of imaginative delusion (5.1.7). In *The Merry Wives of Windsor*, poetry is merely a prop in erotic courtship, as the idiotic Slender wishes that he had brought his copy of *Songs and Sonets* (Tottel's famous *Miscellany*, the first significant anthology of English poetry, published in 1557) to impress the girl he hopes to seduce. In *As You Like It*, Touchstone announces that "the truest poetry is the most feigning," aligning it at once with desire and with lies (3.4.15). In *Julius Caesar*, Brutus asks scornfully about the role of poetry in a world at war: "What should the wars do with these jigging fools?" (4.3.137). We should remember, moreover, that this is the same play in which Cinna the poet is torn apart by a mob who first think he is Cinna the conspirator, and then decide instead to "Tear him for his bad verses" (3.3.28). But poetry is also the chosen medium of heightened speech and solemn emotion in Shakespeare's plays. It sets up the formal expectations that allow Shakespeare to produce such intense, character-driven works. It is also regularly used to close out scenes, as if the gratifying closure of rhyme were the best way to signal the end of an action.

In the non-dramatic poetry, Shakespeare explores various possibilities of literary form, achieving a remarkable marriage of the demands of stanzaic form with the claims of English syntax. The form of *Venus and Adonis* is a six-line stanza, composed of a quatrain followed by a couplet. It is a stanza that is particularly effective at conveying an alternating tension and balance. The quatrain allows for the development and embellishment of an idea, while the couplet gives each stanza a kind of closure; this closure is then opened up, or rendered provisional, in the subsequent stanza. The stanza form of *Lucrece* is rhyme royal, the same form that Chaucer used in *Troilus and Criseyde*; it has one more line than the stanza used in *Venus and Adonis*, added to the quatrain, giving the stanza in essence two couplets. *Lucrece* is almost twice as long as *Venus*, as if this "graver labour" (as Shakespeare termed it in the Dedication) needed more stanzaic space and length to deliberate its weightier subject. This stanza works well to highlight ideas and emotions as they are being worked out, and suits the well-developed inwardness of the two protagonists. Shakespeare returns to this form in "A Lover's Complaint," the poem that follows the Sonnets in the 1609 collection, as if he felt its format was particularly appropriate to the lament of wronged females. In "The Phoenix and Turtle," Shakespeare uses a trochaic tetrameter to convey the poem's enigmatic action. Here, Shakespeare may be revisiting the tetrameter that he had frequently used for various songs in the plays. Indeed, the short lines of this short, odd, gnomic poem provide apt background music for the myriad issues about desire and number that surround the poem.

It is perhaps in the Sonnets that we can best see Shakespeare's remarkable metrical range and lyric virtuosity. The narrow compass of the sonnet

becomes the perfect stage for displaying verbal agility and intellectual ingenuity. Certainly the use of stanzaic form in the narrative poems demonstrates
their formal affinity with the Sonnets; *Venus and Adonis* and *Lucrece* build a
story out of various tightly organized formal units, just as a sonnet sequence
creates expectations of episodic development from the quanta of individual
poems. The remarkable formal virtuosity displayed in the Sonnets may have
been enhanced by Shakespeare's development of the quatrain and the couplet
(ababcc) in *Venus* and of rhyme royal (ababbcc) in *Lucrece*. Both stanzaic forms
begin with a quatrain, and use the couplet to generate closure, so they provide
a good training ground in the building blocks of sonnets.

In 152 sonnets (there are 154 poems, but two exhibit a variant form) composed of three quatrains and a couplet, Shakespeare manages to convey an
amazing range of human experience. The two variants, as we will see, draw
attention to the norm, even as they vary from it significantly. The sonnet
provides the perfect vehicle for a voice engaged in the effort to articulate an
intrinsically unruly desire in socially approved forms and metrically accept-
able ways. Like the protagonists in a Shakespearean comedy, the speakers of
the poems try to synchronize a desire they can only partially control with
circumstances and expectations beyond their control. The typical Shakespeare
sonnet is made up of three quatrains, or four-line stanzas, followed by a couplet that summarizes or revises what was said in the first twelve lines. The
rhyme scheme of a Shakespearean sonnet – *ababcdcdefefgg* – is somewhat less
demanding of a wide range of rhyme words than the form used by Sidney (typically *abbaabbacdcdee*), which is useful in a language such as English. The three
quatrains also prove effective for argument and rumination. A typical Shakespearean sonnet will employ terms of argumentative transition (e.g., when,
then, but) at the beginnings of a quatrain or couplet. After three quatrains
where all rhymes are separated by a line, the proximate rhyme of the couplet
bestows the aural effect of epigrammatic wisdom that lends closure to the
poem.

Shakespeare's poetic line is based less upon rigid syllable counts than on a
careful arrangement of stresses within an understood metrical norm, as one
might expect from a poet who had written both for the theater and for the page.
It aspires to set up expectations that it deliberately either fulfills or frustrates.
Throughout all of Shakespeare's poetry abides a dynamic antagonism between
the halter of form and the spur of emotion. The Sonnets will sometimes
dilate a subject for twelve lines before tying it up, or turning it over, in the
couplet. Shakespeare indeed possesses a remarkable capacity to unfold and
then overturn a position, either in the couplet or in the next poem. Perhaps

this ability to imagine various perspectives helped make him such an effective playwright, since every character in his plays is allowed a significant voice, even if it contradicts other voices. This trait, which played so well on the stage, is also likely what attracted Shakespeare both to the sonnet and to the sonnet cycle, since the process of exploring one side of an issue, and then another, is perfect both for the individual sonnet, and for the relationship between sonnets.

It is telling that the same process of dilation and summation or renunciation occurs, but at a heightened speed, in the stanzas that constitute *Venus* and *Lucrece*. When he wants music, Shakespeare makes the line flow with a kind of gratifying regularity. It is easy for modern readers to miss the effort that produces such music. In his prefatory poem to the First Folio of Shakespeare's plays, though, Ben Jonson, a fellow poet and playwright, praises Shakespeare for his "well toned, and true-filed lines." Jonson knows the immense art required to file the rough matter of language and the refractory substance of passion into metrically regular verse.

Shakespeare, in other words, frequently embeds the intense drama of his poetry in a mellifluous form that belies its often turgid content. His lyric poetry is not as overtly dramatic as that of his contemporary John Donne, whose poems aspire to the rough staccato immediacy of dramatic utterance. Shakespeare by contrast achieves in his sonnets a remarkable confluence of syntax and form that can sometimes seem to mute rather than amplify the drama implicit in the poetry. This surface smoothness – a valued effect in Shakespeare's day – should not lead us to underestimate the drama that seethes under the apparently placid surface.

Throughout his career, Shakespeare aspires to develop a metrical norm which he then plays with subtly or disturbs aggressively. It is typical of the aesthetic sophistication of his formal choices that he uses one of the most metrically regular lines in his entire corpus to inaugurate the poem in which he most self-consciously plays with the idea of convention: "My mistress' eyes are nothing like the sun" (Sonnet 130). Meter here serves as a kind of counterpoint to his lavish and gently comic description of an unconventional mistress:

> My mistress' eyes are nothing like the sun;
> Coral is far more red than her lips' red;
> If snow be white, why then her breasts are dun;
> If hairs be wires, black wires grow on her head.
> I have seen roses damasked, red and white,
> But no such roses see I in her cheeks,
> And in some perfumes is there more delight

> Than in the breath that from my mistress reeks.
> I love to hear her speak, yet well I know
> That music hath a far more pleasing sound;
> I grant I never saw a goddess go –
> My mistress when she walks treads on the ground.
> And yet, by heaven, I think my love as rare
> As any she belied with false compare.

The pendular first line is followed by a largely irregular second line; the poem's metrics cleverly perform the poem's meaning, which is to praise a mistress by suggesting that she varies from the same norms of poetic praise the poem invokes. This delightful poem suggests that the litany of Petrarchan clichés – eyes like suns, cheeks like roses, etc. – is most effective when invoked in order to be disavowed. The regularity of the concluding couplet provides apt background music for the poem's final gesture, which is to practice just the kind of comparison it has ostensibly disavowed.

When he writes a poem about his love for an androgynous young man, though, Shakespeare cleverly chooses to compose the entire poem in the unstressed end rhyme known as "feminine rhyme":

> A woman's face with Nature's own hand painted
> Hast thou, the master-mistress of my passion;
> A woman's gentle heart, but not acquainted
> With shifting change, as is false women's fashion;
> An eye more bright than theirs, less false in rolling,
> Gilding the object whereupon it gazeth;
> A man in hue, all hues in his controlling,
> Which steals men's eyes and women's souls amazeth.
> And for a woman wert thou first created,
> Till Nature as she wrought thee fell a-doting,
> And by addition me of thee defeated,
> By adding one thing to my purpose nothing.
> But since she pricked thee out for women's pleasure,
> Mine be thy love, and thy love's use their treasure.

We will examine Sonnet 20 in more detail in chapter 6. Right now, it is enough to observe that the poem uses a particularly effective blend of meter and rhyme to tell the story of a young man who started out as a woman, but who was endowed with a penis by Nature after Nature began doting on her. The poem's dizzying metamorphoses suggest that perhaps sexual identity based in the addition of a "thing," a penis, is as arbitrary, and as artful, as the addition of a syllable to a line of poetry.

Sonnet 87 also uses feminine rhymes in all but two lines. In this poem, though, the effect is very different; here, the extra syllable produces the lugubrious effect of a dying fall, which suits well the poem's valedictory message:

> Farewell, thou art too dear for my possessing,
> And like enough thou know'st thy estimate:
> The charter of thy worth gives thee releasing;
> My bonds in thee are all determinate.
> For how do I hold thee but by thy granting,
> And for that riches where is my deserving?
> The cause of this fair gift in me is wanting,
> And so my patent back again is swerving.
> Thy self thou gav'st, thy own worth then not knowing,
> Or me, to whom thou gav'st it, else mistaking;
> So thy great gift, upon misprision growing,
> Comes home again, on better judgement making.
> Thus have I had thee, as a dream doth flatter,
> In sleep a king, but waking no such matter.

The financial and legal terminology that suffuses the poem ("dear," "charter," "bonds," "patent") demonstrates the tension between the emotional connection that painfully lingers and the rational claim that is being surrendered.

Meter, then, serves as a remarkable resource for Shakespeare. At its best, his poetry is capable of finding exactly the right music for the sentiment he wishes to convey. When he wants to convey frustration or disgust, moreover, Shakespeare writes lines which are as ponderous and unmusical as possible; in Sonnet 129, for example, he brilliantly characterizes the morally negative causes and the dire consequences of headlong lust through a clogged, halting rhythm:

> Lust
> Is perjured, murd'rous, bloody, full of blame,
> Savage, extreme, rude, cruel, not to trust.

> (lines 2–4)

To attempt to read that last line as even a variant of an iambic pentameter is to experience in one's mouth and ear the expressive force of Shakespeare's metrics. The line brilliantly resists metrical expectation, just as the poem describes a passion which chafes against moral regulation.

A very different kind of metrical accomplishment is achieved in "The Phoenix and Turtle." In this poem, Shakespeare uses a trochaic (a foot composed of a stressed syllable followed by an unstressed syllable – an inverted iamb) tetrameter (four feet per line) to describe the poem's action, perhaps revisiting or revising the tetrameter that he had used for stage songs. Indeed, most of the lines have seven rather than eight syllables, and begin and end with a stressed syllable, leaving the reader to feel the need for one more beat that is not there:

> Let the bird of loudest lay,
> On the sole Arabian tree,
> Herald and sad trumpet be,
> To whose sound chaste wings obey.

This metrical tour de force works well for a poem about the transcendent mysteries of love and desire. We will in a later chapter talk about how this metrical pattern provides appropriate background music for the myriad issues that suffuse the poem's exploration of the mutual individuality of love. For now, it is enough to note Shakespeare's remarkable metrical range and virtuosity in finding effective metrical media for the various moods and ideas he wants to convey.

Shakespeare and early modern poetry

Students are often surprised that Shakespeare, whose reputation as the greatest poet in the language remains largely unchallenged, does not for the most part live up to our contemporary notions of originality. Very few of his dramatic plots are "original" in our modern sense, and several speeches in the plays are taken nearly verbatim from various sources. Shakespeare's originality is not the product of spontaneous imaginative composition (perhaps it never is) but rather a catalytic transformation of found material. Shakespeare possesses a remarkable capacity to absorb the works of others, metabolize them, and produce something better. In each of the genres this book explores, Shakespeare was not a pioneer so much as an irreverent but highly creative follower. He loved to enter well-established genres, and outdo those who had gone before.

There is perhaps something of a competitive streak in this, which finds partial voice in a series of sonnets about rival poets. His *Venus and Adonis* is far superior to the preceding work that created the market for erotic narrative poems based on Ovid – Thomas Lodge's *Scillaes Metamorphosis* (1589) – and is at least as good as a work that emerges almost simultaneously, Marlowe's *Hero and Leander* (1593; we are not sure which comes first, but Marlowe's poem is unfinished). The dedication to *Venus and Adonis,* moreover, promises "some graver labour" to the patron, as if Shakespeare is already planning to outdo himself in the genre, an effort that would produce *Lucrece* (1594) a year later. "The Phoenix and Turtle" in many ways sounds like nothing else in English poetry, but it does have the philosophical seriousness and erotic idealization of John Donne's "The Canonization" or "A Valediction: Forbidding Mourning." The Latin epigraph that Shakespeare chose to preface *Venus and Adonis,* his self-conscious entry into print, is translated as "Let the common herd be amazed by worthless things; but for me let golden Apollo provide cups full of the water of the Muses." With this Latin epigraph, Shakespeare announces at once his knowledge of the classical past and his aspiration to produce uncommonly good verse.

We are not sure when individual sonnets were composed, much less whether Shakespeare ever intended to publish the collection as a sequence, but Shakespeare's sonnet collection was published more than ten years after the great sonnet fad of the 1590s. Inspired by Sir Philip Sidney's popular sequence *Astrophil and Stella,* which was published in 1591, five years after Sidney's tragic death, the sonnet became one of the primary genres of early modern English poetry. For the next ten years, almost any English poet worth his salt produced a sonnet sequence, resulting in literally hundreds of such collections. A twenty-first-century reader can see little variety in them – most tell the story of an abject male's unsuccessful courtship of a distant female in a series of interconnected fourteen-line poems. It is possible that the genre's popularity derived in part from the historical circumstances of the 1590s. Perhaps the presence of Queen Elizabeth, an aging female monarch who liked to be courted and flattered in terms borrowed from erotic poetry, may have made the genre attractive as a kind of rehearsal for a career at court.[4]

Amid the rather strict conventions of this literary fashion, Shakespeare's sequence is not only belated but also highly unusual. Readers familiar with the conventions of sonnet sequences would have approached Shakespeare's volume expecting something similar to what they had come to know. And they would have been shocked to discover themselves in a very different, although not completely alien, genre. Instead of a distant female, the first 126 poems address a beautiful aristocratic male, and even when a female becomes the object of desire in the last poems, she is known for her sexual availability to the speaker and others, not for her chastity. For Shakespeare, the essence of literary accomplishment was in what the Renaissance called "imitation," mastering known genres rather than inventing new ones.

Indeed, imitation invariably elicits various forms of rivalry, all of which suffuse the Sonnets. Rivalry is for Shakespeare both an erotic and an aesthetic issue. While various poems describe rivals for the attentions of a young man or a dark lady, other poems depict Shakespeare's rivalry with other poets.

Indeed, in Sonnet 21, Shakespeare even makes his relationship to other poets a subject of his poetry. He wants first of all to express his deep awareness of the conventions he deliberately disturbs. The sonnet at once shows his anxiety about his relation to his contemporaries and predecessors, and the righteous aggression with which he attempts to assuage this anxiety:

> So is it not with me as with that Muse,
> Stirred by a painted beauty to his verse,
> Who heaven itself for ornament doth use,
> And every fair with his fair doth rehearse,
> Making a couplement of proud compare
> With sun and moon, with earth and sea's rich gems,
> With April's first-born flowers, and all things rare
> That heaven's air in this huge rondure hems.
> O let me, true in love, but truly write,
> And then believe me, my love is as fair
> As any mother's child, though not so bright
> As those gold candles fixed in heaven's air:
> Let them say more that like of hearsay well,
> I will not praise that purpose not to sell.

Shakespeare compares himself favorably here to poets who use exorbitant forms of praise to flatter a lover who is the product of cosmetic enhancement ("painted beauty"). It is as if the inauthenticity of the exorbitant praise he disavows – invoking heavenly light as merely an ornament in comparison to the lover – is matched by the inauthenticity of the beloved. Shakespeare, by contrast, truly loves a lover who is truly fair. He concludes by impugning the mercenary motives of other poets, who, it seems, write only "to sell."

In Sonnet 76, by contrast, the speaker worries about his inability to produce novelty in his verse:

> Why is my verse so barren of new pride?
> So far from variation or quick change?
> Why with the time do I not glance aside
> To new-found methods and to compounds strange?
> Why write I still all one, ever the same,
> And keep invention in a noted weed,
> That every word doth almost tell my name,
> Showing their birth, and where they did proceed?
> O know, sweet love, I always write of you,
> And you and love are still my argument;
> So all my best is dressing old words new,
> Spending again what is already spent:

> For as the sun is daily new and old,
> So is my love still telling what is told.

"Pride," of course, is a largely negative term, so the issue is somewhat loaded from the outset. The three "Why"s that begin lines 1, 3, and 5 signal the speaker's frustration with his inability to write "with the time," but the suggestion of temporizing paves the way for the conclusion, in which the speaker's inability is made a virtue. With the turn from lament to affirmation at line 9 – "O know, sweet love" – the poem divides into an octave and sestet, a form atypical of Shakespeare, but typical of his predecessors in the sonnet.

The poem succeeds, then, by transforming the aesthetic monotony the poem laments into the ethical virtue of constancy the poem praises. The problem it brings up, though – how to create variety amid constancy – abides throughout the sequence. In order to appreciate fully Shakespeare's poetry, we must take note of the immense challenge facing a poet who writes extensive stanzaic poetry or a collection of sonnets – how to satisfy a reader's expectations repeatedly without being predictable and boring. Part of the art is in seeing how many times you can say the same thing, in the same form, freshly. We glimpse something of this phenomenon in the first seventeen of the Sonnets, each of which in a different way encourages the Young Man to procreate. Writing a sonnet sequence is finally a challenge with aesthetic, ethical, and erotic dimensions. Shakespeare inherits an aesthetic emphasizing variety and tries to merge this with an erotic ethic stressing constancy. The challenge of the Sonnets, and of all stanzaic poetry, is at once aesthetic and ethical – how to be constant and faithful without being dull or monotonous.

As a result, the Sonnets develop a dynamic dialectic between aspiration and limitation, between anticipation and frustration, between constancy and variety. No poem is an island, entire unto itself, a fact which puts great pressure on the poet who aspires to supersede his predecessors and contemporaries. Whereas Sonnet 76 worries about the monotony of poetry, Sonnet 59 frets about a related issue – the novelty of the poet's products:

> If there be nothing new, but that which is,
> Hath been before, how are our brains beguiled,
> Which, labouring for invention, bear amiss
> The second burden of a former child!
> O that recòrd could with a backward look,
> Even of five hundred courses of the sun,
> Show me your image in some àntique book,
> Since mind at first in character was done,
> That I might see what the old world could say

To this composèd wonder of your frame:
Whether we are mended, or whe'er better they,
Or whether revolution be the same.
O sure I am the wits of former days
To subjects worse have given admiring praise.

The poem uses the familiar comparison of poetic composition to giving birth, an image which had been brilliantly used by Shakespeare's predecessor Sir Philip Sidney in the first poem of *Astrophil and Stella*. Sidney's poem, a tour de force of poetic frustration, describes a writing block as a crisis in childbirth:

Thus, great with child to speak, and helpless in my throes,
Biting my truant pen, beating myself for spite,
Fool, said my muse to me, look in thy heart and write.[5]

Whereas Sidney resolves his stalled production through the literary intervention of a Muse who paradoxically encourages him to banish literary convention, Shakespeare instead turns back to the subject of his praise, and makes his difficulty into the occasion of praise. With a winning understatement in the concluding couplet, the speaker dampens his original anxiety about his own lack of novelty.

In Sonnet 106, Shakespeare seems to be thinking about the accomplishments of Edmund Spenser, author of the sonnet sequence entitled *Amoretti* as well as the epic entitled *The Faerie Queene*. Spenser achieves in his verse a remarkable music comprising a deliberately archaic vocabulary (e.g., "wight") and subject ("ladies dead and lovely knights"). Shakespeare in this poem is not so much anxious about Spenser's accomplishment as he is interested in thinking about how those "antique" poets that Spenser imitates would have written about his own beloved:

When in the chronicle of wasted time
I see descriptions of the fairest wights,
And beauty making beautiful old rhyme
In praise of ladies dead and lovely knights,
Then in the blazon of sweet beauty's best,
Of hand, of foot, of lip, of eye, of brow,
I see their àntique pen would have expressed
Even such a beauty as you master now.
So all their praises are but prophecies
Of this our time, all you prefiguring,
And for they looked but with divining eyes
They had not skill enough your worth to sing:

> For we, which now behold these present days,
> Had eyes to wonder, but lack tongues to praise.

Shakespeare imagines that all previous poetry of praise functioned as a prophetic anticipation of Shakespeare's own beloved. This is in many ways how Christianity nervously interpreted the splendors of the Classical past – they were prefigurations of transcendent Christian truths. The sonnet is not religious, but it does use religious structures to locate the poet and his object in time.

Shakespeare, then, assimilated much from the various contemporaries he imitated and exceeded. In one of the best accounts available of Shakespeare's metrics, George Wright suggests that Shakespeare learned from both Sidney and Spenser, even as he produced something that neither could have imagined: "if Shakespeare learned from Sidney the art of emphatic speech as a medium for troubled feeling, from Spenser he probably learned the softness and musical grace that results from the skillful use of Pyrrhic feet."[6] Shakespeare also likely learned from Spenser the ability to develop voluptuous pictures in mellifluous verse – most fully on display in *Venus and Adonis* – and from Sidney the capacity to ruminate and argue wittily in verse.

Throughout his career, Shakespeare is fascinated by the complex thermodynamics of praise. He knows that praise is almost always self-reflexive, displaying the talents of the poet even amid the most deferential postures. He is also suspicious of the motives and tropes of conventional praise. In the poems to the Young Man, he wonders how to praise a figure of conventional if striking beauty in arresting ways. In the sonnets to and about a so-called dark lady he speculates on ways of praising a figure whose appearance belies conventional definitions of beauty. In Sonnet 21, Shakespeare offers a series of comparatively conventional claims about his own unconventional plainness and sincerity. In Sonnet 130, by contrast, Shakespeare asserts that his beloved is worthy of praise despite the fact that she fulfills none of the characteristics of conventional praise; she is not fair, she has dark hair, and, most damning of all, she walks on the ground! As in Sonnet 21, Shakespeare assumes a particular negative relation to poetic tradition, and achieves the aura of authenticity by disavowing its clichés. Shakespeare indeed has great fun with the artificiality of the comparisons endorsed by poetic tradition. The couplet of Sonnet 130 cleverly turns the unidealized humanity of the beloved into the source of her uniqueness, and so succeeds in exactly the game the speaker purportedly disavows – praising the beloved via comparison. With its equivocal reference to the "breath that from my mistress reeks," the poem seems to fulfill the delightfully mistaken statement of Dogberry in *Much Ado about Nothing*, that "Comparisons are odorous" (3.5.13).

The couplet, moreover, asserts the uniqueness of "my love," a phrase which designates, as it does so frequently in Shakespeare, both the speaker's desire and the object of that desire. Shakespeare focuses on this ambiguity repeatedly because he is fascinated by the mutually constitutive relationship between desire and the object of desire. Sonnet 21 suggests that true love requires a true object. Sonnet 130 finds the truth of the beloved in the way she defies conventional beauty. In *As You Like It*, Touchstone cleverly asserts that "the truest poetry is the most feigning" (3.4.14), punning on the assonance of feigning, meaning lying, and faining, meaning desiring. Is the authenticity of poetry a function of the depth of the poet's desire, Shakespeare asks, or is it a measure of the depth of the deception? As if to push this question as far as it can go, *As You Like It* includes examples of embarrassingly bad poetry from Orlando, a true lover – is "the truest poetry," Shakespeare asks, the limping but sincere rhymes that Orlando hangs on trees?

Almost all of Shakespeare's non-dramatic poetry turns on issues related to love and/or lust. Shakespeare is fascinated by the proximity of a love that links us to the angels and a lust that can make us behave like beasts. In *Venus and Adonis*, lust is an amoral force invigorating all creation; in *Lucrece*, it is a predatory drive that destroys self and other; in "The Phoenix and Turtle," it is the mystical process by which two beings become one, and in the process achieve a kind of victory over death. We often forget that the phrase "love poetry" is a near oxymoron, divided between the total abandonment that devout love demands and the fastidious control that metrical, rhymed verse requires. Indeed, there is a tension in all love poetry between the abandonment that emotional commitment requires and the self-conscious control that verse induces.

As we will see, throughout his career Shakespeare explores the different possibilities of erotic verse. In *Venus and Adonis*, he conveys a world imbued with pleasure, in which erotic desire is as natural, and as welcome, as the sun or the grass. He places in this world, however, a young man who really is not ready for love, and who articulates with some force the reasons for waiting. In *Lucrece*, a work deliberately counterpoised to the fulsome sensuality of *Venus and Adonis*, Shakespeare explores the destruction of self and other incumbent on the acting-out of unregulated desire; the rape is seen as a brief, supremely unsatisfying act that destroys a woman, causes the exile of the rapist, and brings down a monarchy. The Sonnets will deliberately run the gamut of erotic emotion from tender intimacy and headlong abandonment into fastidious self-control. In doing so, they will explore the provisional and unsatisfying nature of various erotic attitudes. In *A Lover's Complaint*, we will hear the voice of the devastated victim of erotic courtship, and we will also hear her confess that she would willingly do it all again. Finally, in "The Phoenix and Turtle," we will see Shakespeare attempting to find the right voice, somewhere between incantation and conversation, for depicting the mysterious unity achieved by two true lovers, and the mysterious relationship of that ephemeral desire to eternity.

A book like this should dare to answer a question that today's students ask a lot, and that today's scholars probably don't ask enough: why should we still read this stuff? Shakespeare may not in fact be for all time, despite Ben Jonson's assertions to the contrary. Certainly the non-dramatic poetry has suffered greatly amid changes in critical and social attitudes. Yet even if these poems don't speak equally well to all cultures, there is I would argue something in Shakespeare's remarkable transmutation of the poetic and cultural resources made available to him into something that still speaks to us, 400 years after their composition. Indeed, it is remarkable just how much of our current iconography and vocabulary of erotic experience derives from the love poetry that emerged in Shakespeare's lifetime. Shakespeare's abiding concerns with the gamut of emotions and experiences attendant on erotic desire are relevant to any individual whose relationships regularly traverse hope, fear, wonder, reluctance, confusion, anticipation, suspicion, betrayal, and comfort. I would also argue that the specific subjects of Shakespeare's poetry – ideas of race and color, the relation between same-sex and opposite-sex desire, connections between sex and death, and the sexual power of women – have recently become intellectually and socially central to contemporary life in a way that they were not before. We are perhaps in a particularly privileged position thereby to read and appreciate these remarkable poems.

Curiously less dramatic than John Donne's lyrics, and far less celebratory of the pleasures of the flesh, Shakespeare's poetry explores with rigor and imagination just what systems and structures might be used to understand the self and its myriad contradictory desires.[7] He investigates the disturbing rhythms of desire, satiation, and disgust in poetry that pleases. Shakespeare repeatedly achieves that mysteriously pleasing combination of expectation and surprise that is the essence of music and poetry, and the music of poetry. The music will grab you immediately, and the words will continue to thrill and puzzle for a lifetime. The poetry offers a wide range of pleasures that are eminently available to today's reader. This book is a guide to those pleasures, and begins where Shakespeare inaugurated his publishing career, with *Venus and Adonis*, a poem that unequivocally celebrates the conjunction of verbal and carnal pleasure that is the essence of erotic poetry.

Chapter 2

Shakespeare's banquet of sense

Venus and Adonis

> Sex isn't just friction and shallow fun. Sex is also the revenge on death.
> – Philip Roth, *The Dying Animal*

Always eager to please his audience, Shakespeare wrote a play called *As You Like It*. But before that he wrote a narrative poem as he thought they liked it, and he called it *Venus and Adonis*. He was a young, ambitious writer, hoping to compose a work that would garner both popular and aristocratic attention by pleasing a wide range of literary and erotic tastes. And he succeeded brilliantly. In the dedication, Shakespeare calls it "the first heir of my invention," despite the fact he may have already written as many as seven plays.[1] Clearly, he is announcing his ambition to do something even more significant, and imagining this poem as a crucial inauguration in the construction of a literary career. Indeed, the dedication also suggests that if the poem's patron will "seem but pleased," the poet will honor his patron subsequently with "some graver labour." As if this somewhat presumptuous dedication were not ambitious enough, the Latin epigraph – *Vilia miretur vulgus: mihi flavus Apollo / Pocula Castalia plena minister aqua* ("Let base-conceited wits admire vile things, / Fair Phoebus lead me to the Muses' springs") – comes from a poem in which the Classical poet Ovid, whom Shakespeare is purposefully imitating, announces his own literary ambition.

Shakespeare was 29 years old when the poem was first printed in quarto in 1593. It was dedicated to Henry Wriothesley, 3rd Earl of Southampton, who was 20, and under the guardianship of William Cecil until the age of 21. In 1589, Cecil had tried unsuccessfully to arrange a marriage between his granddaughter and Southampton. It is possible that this sensual tale of erotic prurience and resistance absorbed some of these circumstances. We do know that the first poem dedicated to Southampton is John Clapham's Latin poem *Narcissus* in 1591 – a theme with some resemblance to *Venus and Adonis*. It is likely that the theme of rejecting excessive self-regard, and participating instead in the heterosexual economy of marriage and reproduction, had an admonitory application to the handsome young aristocrat. Regardless, it was a brilliant moment in which to dedicate a poem to Southampton, who was about to become a very rich man.

The dedication itself is a piece of artful deference:

> Right Honorable,
>
> I know not how I shall offend in dedicating my unpolished lines to your Lordship, nor how the world will censure me for choosing so strong a prop to support so weak a burden. Only if your Honour seem but pleased, I account myself highly praised, and vow to take advantage of all idle hours, till I have honoured you with some graver labour. But if the first heir of my invention prove deformed, I shall be sorry it had so noble a godfather, and never after ear so barren a land for fear it yield me still so bad a harvest. I leave it to your Honourable survey, and your Honour to your heart's content, which I wish may always answer your own wish, and the world's hopeful expectation.
>
> Your Honour's in all duty,
>
> William Shakespeare.

"Unpolished lines" is one of the least apt descriptions one can imagine for this highly polished poem, yet part of the deferential art of the courtier-poet is to call attention through disavowal to exactly those traits that one wants the reader to notice. Shakespeare locates his definition of success not in the opinion of "the world" but rather in the degree to which he has pleased his potential patron. He also promises that he will offer to Southampton "some graver labour," premised on the unstated proposition of the patron's beneficence. This promise was fulfilled a year later with the publication of *Lucrece*, a longer and much more solemn poem.

Venus and Adonis was immensely successful and regularly reprinted, six times in the next seven years. In all, it appeared in seventeen editions before 1641. It was Shakespeare's most popular work during his lifetime, and it was the poem most cited by Shakespeare's contemporaries. Since Shakespeare followed the poem with *Lucrece* a year later, also dedicated to Southampton, we can assume the poem's plea for patronage met with some success. Indeed, Southampton is one of the many candidates for the mysterious "Mr. W. H." to whom the Sonnets are dedicated, since "W. H." is a transposed version of his initials.

There is, however, no evidence of a relationship with Southampton after the publication of *Lucrece* in 1594.

The source for Shakespeare's poem is Ovid's *Metamorphoses*, Book 10. Ovid had been popular in England for quite a while. Ovid was, moreover, a central part of the curriculum in sixteenth-century grammar schools; schoolboys such as Shakespeare would have been required to do extensive reading, memorizing, and translating of the poet. Ovid had been translated into English, moreover, in 1567 by Arthur Golding.[2] Ovid, though, devotes just 85 lines to the story, while Shakespeare gives it almost 1,200. Ovid's Adonis, moreover, is far less reluctant to respond to Venus' seduction, although he does meet the same unfortunate end.

Ovid fascinated Shakespeare, because the *Metamorphoses* in particular allowed Shakespeare to think through just what kind of beings we become when we surrender to or deny our passions. The story of Venus and Adonis allowed Shakespeare to explore a situation which reversed the conventional expectations of gender and status. In this case, it is not a distant reluctant woman who resists the seductions of a male courtier – the standard romance plot – but rather a lusty older goddess who courts a much younger man. There is a somewhat derogatory term current in American popular culture for older women who associate socially with younger men – cougars. Shakespeare would have been sympathetic; his Venus is the original cougar, a predatory female who feeds "glutton-like" on "the yielding prey," a reluctant, adolescent male (*Venus*, lines 547–58).

Carnal and verbal pleasure

If the dedication is unembarrassed about the literary ambitions of its author, the poem is unembarrassed about the sensual pleasure championed by its central female character. This is not a poem to which moralists have responded well; C. S. Lewis was in many ways at his worst when he asserted that "If the poem is not meant to arouse disgust it was very foolishly written."[3] As we will see, Shakespeare will have his moments of ethical disgust with sexuality, but they are not in *Venus and Adonis*; in fact, disgust is probably the last feeling the poem intends to arouse. Rather, the poem describes male and female bodies as objects of immense beauty and erotic interest. The poem includes a delicate but delightfully volatile mixture of wit and eroticism, of humor and desire. Eros is viewed as a power that we resist at our peril. The poem brilliantly merges erotic titillation with the sensual pleasures of verse, allowing these two kinds of pleasure to reinforce each other. At a strategic moment in the seduction, Titan the sun-god watches and wishes he could be in Adonis' place; Titan:

> With burning eye did hotly overlook them,
> Wishing Adonis had his team to guide,
> So he were like him and by Venus' side.
>
> (lines 178–80)

This is I think how many of Shakespeare's male and female readers would have responded to the poem, inserting themselves into one or more subject positions that they found satisfying. Adonis' reluctance is less a moral stance than the occasion for further erotic pressures from Venus, pressures to which the reader would respond, even if Adonis does not.

Indeed, the poem seems to have developed a reputation for salacious content. In 1598, a character in a Cambridge play indicates that the poem might function as an aid to solitary pleasure, promising to "worship sweet Mr. Shakspeare," and to "lay his Venus and Adonis under my pillow."[4] In the second part of this play, a character praises the sensual experience of Shakespeare's poetry, but wishes that Shakespeare would write about more serious issues:

> Who loues not *Adons* loue, or *Lucrece* rape?
> His sweeter verse contaynes hart throbbing line,
> Could but a grauer subiect him content,
> Without loues foolish lazy languishment.[5]

In *A Mad World, My Masters* by Thomas Middleton (a play first performed in 1605 and published in 1608), a jealous and soon-to-be-cuckolded character named Harebrain confiscates *Venus and Adonis* as well as Marlowe's *Hero and Leander* from his wife because he is afraid of the effect such literature might have: "I have convey'd away all her wanton pamphlets, as Hero and Leander, Venus and Adonis; Oh, two luscious mary-bone pies for a young married wife."[6] The phallic connotations of a pie made from marrow-bones suit well the lubricious textures of the poem. Sir John Davies is almost certainly thinking of Shakespeare when in 1610 he imagines the moralized voice of paper complaining about women reading in private a poem about Venus and Adonis:

> Another (ah Lord helpe) mee vilifies
> With Art of Loue, and how to subtilize,
> Making lewd *Venus*, with eternall Lines,
> To tye *Adonis* to her loues designes:
> Fine wit is shew'n therein: but finer twere
> If not attired in such bawdy Geare.
> But be it as it will: the coyest Dames,

> In priuate read it for their Closset-games:
> For, sooth to say, the Lines so draw them on,
> To the venerian speculation,
> That will they, nill they (if of flesh they bee)
> They will thinke of it, sith loose Thought is free.[7]

Certainly, *Venus and Adonis* was thought to possess a great erotic charge that appealed to a wide range of tastes and desires.

Much of its popularity indeed may stem in part from its successful marriage of prurient surfaces and gorgeous poetry. Relatedly, the poem offers a fascinating series of reversals of conventional courtship situations, which are intellectually and erotically engaging. Instead of a male courting a distant female, we watch a sexually aggressive goddess court an adolescent male. The poem repeatedly suggests that love by its very nature is unruly, defying conventional circumstances and overturning standard hierarchies. Venus brags to Adonis that she has been the object of just the kind of seductive attention that she is now devoting to Adonis:

> I have been wooed, as I entreat thee now,
> Even by the stern and direful god of war,
> Whose sinewy neck in battle ne'er did bow,
> Who conquers where he comes in every jar;
> Yet hath he been my captive and my slave,
> And begged for that which thou unasked shalt have.
>
> Over my altars hath he hung his lance,
> His batter'd shield, his uncontrollèd crest,
> And for my sake hath learned to sport and dance,
> To toy, to wanton, dally, smile and jest,
> Scorning his churlish drum and ensign red,
> Making my arms his field, his tent my bed.
> Thus he that overruled I overswayèd,
> Leading him prisoner in a red-rose chain;
> Strong-tempered steel his stronger strength obeyèd,
> Yet was he servile to my coy disdain.
>
> (lines 97–112)

Venus has herself been the occasion for the inversion of conventional hierarchies, entertaining the attentions of the gods. Even Mars, the hyper-masculine god of war, was rendered servile by her coy disdain. Part of the pleasure of the poem derives from our fascination at the scenario of the queen of love made subject to the same irrational forces that she embodies. We also relish watching the display of sheer appetite and pleasure, particularly when it is situated in a woman who courts a reluctant male. Some of the sweet irony of Venus' situation is embedded in the various complex meanings of the word "love": "She's love, she loves, and yet she is not loved" (line 610).

In *Venus and Adonis*, Shakespeare explores the power of Eros to make humans and gods behave foolishly. This is of course a theme that runs through many of Shakespeare's dramatic comedies as well. Yet despite the subordinating folly to which love can drive us, Shakespeare does not in *Venus and Adonis* endorse the repudiation of love. Rather, as in his early comedy *Love's Labour's Lost*, Shakespeare shows how the disavowal of love can become a kind of foreplay that prolongs rather than denies desire. Adonis' resistance seems somewhat out of place in a world seething with sensuality. Yet it is also necessary for the full articulation of Venus' seduction. It would be a different poem, less interesting and perhaps even less erotic, if Adonis were a willing partner.

Wordplay and foreplay

Indeed, Venus' rhetorical inventiveness is a central element of her erotic attraction. Wordplay is a kind of foreplay in the world of the poem. As Venus promises Adonis, "Bid me discourse, I will enchant thine ear" (line 145). Shakespeare's language in this poem is highly patterned, and designed to advertise those patterns. The language is seeded with the various rhetorical schemes that Shakespeare would have learned in grammar school, and at times it seems as if he might still be trying to impress that Stratford schoolmaster. Among the many rhetorical devices that the poem repeatedly deploys are parison (parallel phrases), isocolon (phrases of equal length and grammar), antimetabole (phrases repeated in inverted order), epanalepsis (phrases repeated at the beginning and ending of the line). It is the work of a poet who is trying to display how much he knows and what he can do with this knowledge. Perhaps this can be understood as a reaction to the understandable insecurity a writer would feel about his first publication. But Shakespeare is also working to the demands of a popular aesthetic, which suggested that the pleasure we take in an utterance is measured by the degree of its embellishment. In this aesthetic, adjectives are asked to do much of the work. Indeed, when one adjective will not do, Shakespeare repeatedly calls upon compound adjectives. The opening stanza of *Venus and Adonis* exemplifies the burden of description that adjectives are repeatedly asked to carry in this poem:

> Even as the sun with purple-coloured face
> Had tane his last leave of the weeping morn,

> Rose-cheeked Adonis hied him to the chase;
> Hunting he loved, but love he laughed to scorn.
> Sick-thoughted Venus makes amain unto him,
> And like a bold-faced suitor gins to woo him.

It is almost as if the irrepressible erotic energies of creation lead even the adjectives to pair off.

Venus' desire makes her "Sick-thoughted," as if the discomfort of unsatisfied desire possessed its own pathology. Desire is indeed often described in Shakespeare as a kind of disease. As we will see in subsequent chapters, Shakespeare is troubled by the very different illnesses produced by desire indulged and consummated. But, in *Venus and Adonis*, Shakespeare emphasizes only the profound discomfort of desire suppressed. Venus' inaugural discomfort will be surpassed by the fatal wound that the rejection of love will indirectly inflict on Adonis.

Like a typical Renaissance love poet, Venus begins her courtship with flattery, but the particular form it takes is appropriate only to her and would be deeply indecorous in others "Thrice fairer than myself" (line 7). The line reminds us, as the poem does continually, of the structural irony by which the goddess of love is made subject to the forces of love. It also reminds us of the way that desire for another can be grounded in narcissism or competitive with it.

Shakespeare is in this poem fascinated by the phenomenon of erotic appetite, wondering what arouses it, and what might sate it. Venus entices Adonis with the prelapsarian prospect of continual arousal, a paradise without a serpent:

> Here come and sit, where never serpent hisses,
> And being set, I'll smother thee with kisses;
> And yet not cloy thy lips with loathed satiety,
> But rather famish them amid their plenty.
>
> (lines 17–20)

The verbs that cluster around Venus' actions, though, are telling: here she "smother[s]" him, and in a few lines she "seizeth" his hand. There is in her approach a kind of desperate aggression, even violence, for all of its talk of love and pleasure.

There is a curious eruption of alliteration as she takes his hand, as if Shakespeare were absorbing the archaic aesthetic of an earlier mode of English poetry:

> With this she seizeth on his sweating palm,
> The precedent of pith and livelihood,

> And trembling in her passion calls it balm,
> Earth's sovereign salve to do a goddess good.
>
> (lines 25–28)

Perhaps because the two protagonists are about to get on horseback, the poem starts sounding briefly like an alliterative medieval romance. Adonis' "sweating palm" signifies an amorous nature in Elizabethan lore; the detail seems to indicate that Adonis' body is not fully in agreement with his resisting mind.

As Venus carries Adonis away, we are allowed both to see the full "force" of her desire, and to laugh at the deeply comic scenario of a pouting adolescent under the arm of a goddess:

> Being so enraged, desire doth lend her force
> Courageously to pluck him from his horse.
>
> Over one arm the lusty courser's rein,
> Under her other was the tender boy,
> Who blushed and pouted in a dull disdain,
> With leaden appetite, unapt to toy:
> She red and hot as coals of glowing fire,
> He red for shame, but frosty in desire.
>
> (lines 29–36)

Both amorous goddess and reluctant adolescent exhibit a ruddy complexion, but Shakespeare gives us the polar-opposite motives for their superficial similarity: she is red hot with passion, while he burns with shame. Yet by calling attention to their resemblance, Shakespeare hints at the tacit connections between shame and the desire it elicits. The poem is a study in scarlet and white; throughout the poem, the palette of red and white signals heightened erotic interest. Shakespeare develops an elaborate counterpointing of the two colours.

Venus uses various forms of verbal and physical coercion as she attempts to seduce Adonis. At one moment, she begins to sound as though she has been reading the opening poems of Shakespeare's Sonnets, in which the speaker urges a narcissistic young man to reproduce:

> Is thine own heart to thine own face affected?
> Can thy right hand seize love upon thy left?
> Then woo thyself, be of thyself rejected;
> Steal thine own freedom, and complain on theft.
> Narcissus so himself himself forsook,
> And died to kiss his shadow in the brook.
> Torches are made to light, jewels to wear,

> Dainties to taste, fresh beauty for the use,
> Herbs for their smell, and sappy plants to bear:
> Things growing to themselves are growth's abuse:
> Seeds spring from seeds and beauty breedeth beauty;
> Thou wast begot; to get it is thy duty.
> Upon the earth's increase why shouldst thou feed,
> Unless the earth with thy increase be fed?
> By law of nature thou art bound to breed,
> That thine may live when thou thyself art dead;
> And so in spite of death thou dost survive,
> In that thy likeness still is left alive.   (lines 157–74)

By accusing him of narcissism, Venus not only invokes another Ovidian tale – that of Narcissus – but also implies that love of self is one of the few possible explanations for rejecting the goddess of love. She even suggests that love has a kind of necessary ecological function; because Adonis is fed by a nature that is premised on reproduction, his refusal to participate in that reproductive process is hypocritical, and ultimately self-defeating.

Venus has an almost palpable physical presence in the poem. She continually foregrounds her body as if its various sites of pleasure were a central aspect of the poem's ecology of love. At one point, she offers a blazon of her own beauty, enumerating her various attractions:

> Thou canst not see one wrinkle in my brow,
> Mine eyes are grey and bright and quick in turning,
> My beauty as the spring doth yearly grow,
> My flesh is soft and plump, my marrow burning.
> My smooth moist hand, were it with thy hand felt,
> Would in thy palm dissolve, or seem to melt.
>
> (lines 139–44)

Her "moist hand" matches Adonis' "sweating palm" (line 25), and promises or threatens to dissolve with his in passion. In one of the most overtly erotic passages in this highly erotic poem, Venus uses the conventional pun on deer/dear to offer Adonis the chance to feed on the lush landscape of her body:

> I'll be a park, and thou shalt be my deer:
> Feed where thou wilt, on mountain or in dale;
> Graze on my lips, and if those hills be dry,
> Stray lower, where the pleasant fountains lie.
>
> Within this limit is relief enough,
> Sweet bottom-grass and high delightful plain,
> Round rising hillocks, brakes obscure and rough,

> To shelter thee from tempest and from rain:
> Then be my deer, since I am such a park,
> No dog shall rouse thee, though a thousand bark.
>
> (lines 231–40)

Although this graphic description has little apparent effect on Adonis – he only "smiles as in disdain" (line 241) – one can imagine that it exercised greater power over the average reader of the time, unaccustomed to such detailed representations of female anatomy. The deer/dear pun, moreover, reminds us of this tale's origin in Ovid's *Metamorphoses*, a text whose various stories of transformation depict the way that lust makes beasts of gods and humans alike.

As if to drive home Adonis' aberrant refusal of what Venus calls "the laws of nature," Adonis' horse breaks loose, and "courts" another horse. A more moralistic poet such as Edmund Spenser would use this episode to depict the inherent beastliness of the lust to which Venus attempts to draw Adonis. But Shakespeare, by contrast, uses the episode to make Adonis look out of step with the world he inhabits. It is as if the environment of the poem were in conspiracy with Venus; Adonis appears to be resisting not just Venus' seductions but rather some universal life principle, located in a realm beyond morality. Just as Adonis is about to ride his horse away, the animal is distracted by another horse:

> from forth a copse that neighbours by,
> A breeding jennet, lusty, young and proud,
> Adonis' trampling courser doth espy,
> And forth she rushes, snorts and neighs aloud.
> The strong-necked steed, being tied unto a tree,
> Breaketh his rein, and to her straight goes he.
>
> (lines 259–64)

Shakespeare relishes the poetic challenge of describing animal desire, and the opportunity for phallic puns that it makes available: "His ears up-pricked, his braided hanging mane / Upon his compassed crest now stand on end" (lines 271–72). This is physical excitement of a particularly masculine kind. As if to underscore the point, the word "proud" is used three times in forty lines (260, 288, 300), emphasizing the sexual display that is at the root of the term.

For Shakespeare the horse represents a force that is normally pent up but is now let loose: "The iron bit he crusheth 'tween his teeth, / Controlling what he was controllèd with" (lines 269–70). Shakespeare is fascinated by the intricate dance of animal courtship, and the ways it can be seen to comment on the patterns and conventions of human courtship. Shakespeare comically imagines that Adonis' horse experiences a version of the monomania that motivates human lovers: "He sees his love, and nothing else he sees / For nothing else with his proud sight agrees" (lines 287–88). The female jennet, in turn, becomes a kind of coy mistress:

> He looks upon his love and neighs unto her,
> She answers him as if she knew his mind;
> Being proud, as females are, to see him woo her,
> She puts on outward strangeness, seems unkind,
> Spurns at his love and scorns the heat he feels,
> Beating his kind embracements with her heels.
>
> (lines 307–12)

Adonis' horse responds like a human male, reacting to his lover's disdain with sadness:

> Then like a melancholy malcontent
> He vails his tail that, like a falling plume
> Cool shadow to his melting buttock lent;
> He stamps, and bites the poor flies in his fume.
> His love, perceiving how he was enraged,
> Grew kinder, and his fury was assuaged.
>
> (lines 313–18)

Shakespeare intends for us to laugh here, but not in a way that emphasizes our superiority to the animals. Rather we realize that our patterns of courtship are simply glorified versions of animal behavior. As the two horses go off into the woods to "mak[e] the beast with two backs," to borrow a phrase from *Othello* (1.1.128), it is Adonis, "All swoln with chafing" rather than with the pleasurable tumescence of sexual desire, who becomes the butt of laughter.

Indeed, if we miss the point that the horses provide a model for human erotic behavior, Shakespeare's highly articulate Venus is there to drive it home:

> Thy palfrey, as he should,
> Welcomes the warm approach of sweet desire.
> Affection is a coal that must be cooled,
> Else suffered it will set the heart on fire.
> The sea hath bounds, but deep desire hath none;
> Therefore no marvel though thy horse be gone.
> How like a jade he stood tied to the tree,
> Servilely mastered with a leathern rein;
> But when he saw his love, his youth's fair fee,
> He held such petty bondage in disdain,

> Throwing the base thong from his bending crest,
> Enfranchising his mouth, his back, his breast.
>
> (lines 385–96)

Venus offers here a theory of desire as something sweet and infinite, yet dangerous if not honored and acted upon. It is a fire that cannot be ignored, and that needs to be cooled, it seems, by the vent of sex. It is, moreover, a force that can lead one to political liberation; it encourages Adonis' horse to throw off the "petty bondage" of a "leathern rein."

Venus indeed tells Adonis that he merely needs to learn what his horse already knows:

> O, learn to love; the lesson is but plain,
> And once made perfect, never lost again.
>
> (lines 407–08)

Adonis, though, suggests another beast that might be the object of his "love":

> "I know not love", quoth he, "nor will not know it,
> Unless it be a boar, and then I chase it.
> 'Tis much to borrow, and I will not owe it;
> My love to love is love but to disgrace it,
> For I have heard it is a life in death,
> That laughs and weeps, and all but with a breath"
>
> (lines 409–14)

This is at once awkward and funny – for a moment it seems that Adonis favors love with a boar, until we realize that he is referring to his desire to hunt the boar. But the weirdness lingers, and when Adonis is finally killed by the boar, erotic elements are folded into the human-animal encounter in ways that sustain the discomfort. Projecting her own situation and desire onto the boar, Venus imagines that the boar "thought to kiss him, and hath killed him so" (line 1,110). She proceeds to imagine an even more erotic scenario, by which "the loving swine," "nuzzling in his flank . . . Sheathed unaware the tusk in his soft groin" (lines 1,115–16). Some of the energies of same-sex desire that will animate the Sonnets course through this curious animal-human encounter. Ironically, the bodily area that Adonis has been ignoring – his groin – is the area in which he receives his death wound. Clearly, Adonis' preference for hunting boars over making love with the goddess of love is imagined as a kind of unhealthy transference of suppressed erotic energies. The wound he receives in his groin, moreover, consummates the various forms of violence implicit in Venus' erotic approaches.

Love and lust

Adonis and Venus engage in a brief but telling debate about the nature of love. Adonis is left mainly to say what he has heard, since he has no first-hand knowledge of the emotion. He has been told about the standard contradictions that Petrarchan lovers feel: "I have heard it is a life in death / That laughs and weeps, and all but with a breath" (lines 413–14). Like a Petrarchan lover, Venus describes the agony of her unfulfilled desire, now increased by her apprehension of the sensuous attractions of Adonis' voice:

> Thy mermaid's voice hath done me double wrong;
> I had my load before, now pressed with bearing:
> Melodious discord, heavenly tune harsh sounding,
> Ears' deep-sweet music, and heart's deep sore wounding.
>
> (lines 429–32)

The pressing weight invoked in the second line describes a cruelly slow method of execution in early modern England; weights would be added incrementally to a platform placed on the body until it was crushed. For Venus, this incremental torture is what it is like to be around Adonis, the resistant object of her fervent desire. Yet the image also encapsulates a version of the sexual activity Venus seeks, whereby one body presses on another in intercourse. Venus' agony allows Shakespeare to explore the close relationship between the pleasure that causes one to desire another and the agony that results from this desire being unfulfilled. In so doing, Shakespeare demonstrates the experiential basis of the Petrarchan oxymorons that Adonis innocently invokes.

Venus blazons Adonis' attractions in terms of the five senses to which his being appeals. She praises his "inward beauty and invisible" which would appeal to her "ears," his "outward parts" that would appeal to her eyes, his "touch," and his "very smell," then erupts in enthusiasm for his "taste": "But O what banquet wert thou to the taste, / Being nurse and feeder of the other four" (lines 445–46). Carried away by the literal sensuality of her own language, Venus imagines that the senses would "wish the feast might ever last" (line 447). The eternal banquet of sense that makes up the poem merges with the transient feast of consumable pleasures that Venus projects onto Adonis.

This sensual fantasy, however, is met by Adonis' austere disapproval, and his stern gaze causes her to fall down, as if she has fainted. More physical comedy ensues, as Adonis, thinking he has killed her, scrambles to revive her. The activity is truly funny:

> He wrings her nose, he strikes her on the cheeks,
> He bends her fingers, holds her pulses hard,
> He chafes her lips: a thousand ways he seeks
> To mend the hurt that his unkindness marred.
> He kisses her.   (lines 475–79)

The kiss awakens her, and leads her to ask him to "kill me once again" (line 499). Venus' feigned death offers the occasion for several such puns on the common colloquialism that links dying and sexual climax, and the young Shakespeare does not resist the temptation. It also provides an opportunity for the rehearsal of the emotions that will be aroused by the ultimate death of Adonis.

Indeed, when Adonis tells her that he is to hunt the boar tomorrow, Venus again faints, and the physical comedy blossoms, with a profoundly erotic edge:

> she trembles at his tale,
> And on his neck her yoking arms she throws:
> She sinketh down, still hanging by his neck;
> He on her belly falls, she on her back.
>
> (lines 591–94)

Never one to miss an opportunity for amatory activity, Venus attempts to take advantage of the physical situation:

> Now is she in the very lists of love,
> Her champion mounted for the hot encounter.
> All is imaginary she doth prove;
> He will not manage her, although he mount her: . . .
>
> The warm effects which she in him finds missing
> She seeks to kindle with continual kissing.
>
> (lines 595–606)

Shakespeare likens Adonis to an inept equestrian, and he compares Venus to "poor birds" who "deceived with painted grapes / Do surfeit by the eye, and pine the maw" (lines 601–02). The mismatch is frustrating to both parties, and is encapsulated wonderfully in a line that explodes the various meanings of love that are operative in the poem: "She's love, she loves, and yet she is not loved" (line 610). Even though he knows it will not end well, at least for Adonis, Shakespeare emphasizes the madcap comedy of this situation of mutual frustration.

Indeed, after the physical comedy of their frustrated grappling, the language of the poem begins to darken slightly, particularly as the day comes to an end. Venus adopts the admonitory tone that we will also hear in the Sonnets, warning Adonis to take action against the inevitable ravages of time by having sex in order to procreate:

> What is thy body but a swallowing grave,
> Seeming to bury that posterity
> Which by the rights of time thou needs must have
> If thou destroy them not in dark obscurity?
> If so, the world will hold thee in disdain,
> Sith in thy pride so fair a hope is slain.
> So in thyself thyself art made away,
> A mischief worse than civil home-bred strife,
> Or theirs whose desperate hands themselves do slay,
> Or butcher sire that reaves his son of life.
> Foul cank'ring rust the hidden treasure frets,
> But gold that's put to use more gold begets.
>
> (lines 757–68)

With characteristic hyperbole, Venus suggests that Adonis' refusal to have sex with her is the equivalent of killing himself or his offspring. As in the Sonnets, the concept of "use," loaning money out at interest, exemplifies the implicit economics of heterosexual reproduction, spending the capital of sperm to gain the interest of children.

Like a good dramatist who can ventriloquize all sides of a situation, Shakespeare allows Adonis some significant statements of his own position of resistance. Adonis cleverly plays on the differences between carnal knowledge and self-knowledge, suggesting that if Venus really loved him, she would allow him to grow up before demanding sexual relations with him: "Before I know myself, seek not to know me" (line 525). Adonis also turns the concept of love back upon Venus, offering a sustained attempt to separate the theoretically unselfish emotion of love from the self-indulgent hungers of lust:

> Call it not Love, for Love to heaven is fled
> Since sweating Lust on earth usurped his name,
> Under whose simple semblance he hath fed
> Upon fresh beauty, blotting it with blame;
> Which the hot tyrant stains and soon bereaves,
> As caterpillars do the tender leaves.
>
> Love comforteth like sunshine after rain,
> But Lust's effect is tempest after sun;
> Love's gentle spring doth always fresh remain,

> Lust's winter comes ere summer half be done;
> Love surfeits not, Lust like a glutton dies;
> Love is all truth, Lust full of forgèd lies.
>
> (lines 793–804)

Adonis has a point when he suggests that love is ideally less self-involved than the hedonistic appetites displayed by Venus, although the two experiences rarely sort out as neatly or completely as he suggests. Indeed, his imagery keeps implying that lust is a part of a temporal or meteorological continuum with love – contrasting winter to summer, for example, or tempests to sun – rather than something completely different. His moralizing efforts, moreover, are complicated by the highly conventional, even inert imagery he employs, and by the innate comedy of an inexperienced adolescent lecturing the Goddess of Love about the nature of the emotion she embodies amid a landscape suffused with her own erotic energies.

The death of Adonis and the birth of erotic unhappiness

When Venus first spies the boar, the animal manifests the same palette that Adonis had demonstrated in our first view of him; his "froth mouth bepainted all with red, / Like milk and blood being mingled both together" (lines 901–02). In a kind of erotic consummation, the sputum of the boar mixes with the blood of Adonis. As Venus realizes that the blood indeed is from her beloved Adonis, she experiences a perfect storm of grief and horror:

> Variable passions throng her constant woe,
> As striving who should best become her grief.
> All entertained, each passion labours so
> That every present sorrow seemeth chief.
> But none is best; then join they all together,
> Like many clouds consulting for foul weather.
>
> (lines 967–72)

Shakespeare here is fascinated by the myriad currents of Venus' grief, as if he were rehearsing for the grief-filled poem he would produce the next year, *Lucrece*; in that poem, overt emotional responses to violent devastation will take center stage. In *Venus*, by contrast, Shakespeare tracks the painful mixture of hope and grief that she experiences until she finds the body of Adonis. When she "hears some huntsman halloo," she convinces herself that it is the voice of

Adonis (line 973). This allows Shakespeare to explore the volatile combination of skepticism and credulity that is love:

> O hard-believing Love, how strange it seems,
> Not to believe, and yet too credulous!
> Thy weal and woe are both of them extremes,
> Despair and hope makes thee ridiculous:
> The one doth flatter thee in thoughts unlikely,
> In likely thoughts the other kills thee quickly.
>
> (lines 985–90)

Love, Shakespeare suggests, abides with the extremities of hope and despair.

When Venus discovers the dead body of Adonis, hope evaporates. Shakespeare records the befuddled desolations of grief with a great sense of physical detail.

> Over one shoulder doth she hang her head;
> Dumbly she passions, franticly she doteth,
> She thinks he could not die, he is not dead;
> Her voice is stopped, her joints forget to bow,
> Her eyes are mad that they have wept til now.
>
> (lines 1,058–62)

At the same time, Shakespeare gently reminds us of the self-indulgent nature of her grief. Venus looks at Adonis' eyes, and sees "Two glasses where herself herself beheld / A thousand times" (lines 1,129–30). Even when she looked into his eyes, the proverbial window of his soul, she only saw her own desire for him. It is as if her origins in the deeply self-interested pursuit of pure pleasure make even her sorrow profoundly self-regarding.

Like the petulant, spoiled children that the gods so frequently mimic in Ovid, Venus then decides that if she cannot have her beloved Adonis, no one else can be happy in love.

> Since thou art dead, lo, here I prophesy,
> Sorrow on love hereafter shall attend;
> It shall be waited on with jealousy,
> Find sweet beginning, but unsavoury end;
> Ne'er settled equally, but high or low,
> That all love's pleasure shall not match his woe.
>
> (lines 1,135–40)

The poem then becomes a kind of etiology of the myriad sorrows that accompany love. It also offers a summary of the various plots that a certain young dramatist would soon exploit on the Elizabethan stage:

> It [love] shall be fickle, false and full of fraud,
> Bud, and be blasted, in a breathing while,
> The bottom poison, and the top o'er-strawed
> With sweets that shall the truest sight beguile:
> The strongest body shall it make most weak,
> Strike the wise dumb, and teach the fool to speak.
>
> It shall be sparing, and too full of riot,
> Teaching decrepit age to tread the measures;
> The staring ruffian shall it keep in quiet,
> Pluck down the rich, enrich the poor with treasures;
> It shall be raging mad, and silly mild,
> Make the young old, the old become a child.
>
> It shall suspect where is no cause of fear,
> It shall not fear where it should most mistrust;
> It shall be merciful, and too severe,
> And most deceiving when it seems most just;
> Perverse it shall be where it shows most toward,
> Put fear to valour, courage to the coward.
>
> It shall be cause of war and dire events,
> And set dissension 'twixt the son and sire,
> Subject and servile to all discontents,
> As dry combustious matter is to fire.
> Sith in his prime death doth my love destroy,
> They that love best their loves shall not enjoy.
>
> (lines 1,141–64)

In this catalog of the various forms of unhappiness that love will elicit, we can see the genesis of the plots of Shakespearean comedy, tragedy, and romance. Indeed, in *A Midsummer Night's Dream*, Shakespeare will reprise this catalog of the injuries of love to prove that "The course of true love never did run smooth" (1.1.134–49).

Venus and Adonis, though, also offers the conventional Ovidian consolation of bodily transformation: in this case, the purple flower that springs up from Adonis' spilled blood. Venus plucks the flower, telling the flower that "it is as good / To wither in my breast as in his blood" (lines 1,181–82). Part of the joke of this scene inheres in our recognition that Venus is able to do with the passive flower what she wanted to do with Adonis – pluck it and hold it to her breast. With loud erotic overtones, Venus promises that "There shall not be one minute in an hour / Wherein I will not kiss my sweet love's flower" (lines 1,187–88). Amid the poem's rampant and delicious pleasures, it is easy to forget that this is as close as we get to an actual consummation. Rather, the poem is about the pleasures of titillation, and the various ways that erotic desire is dispersed and aroused by all of the five senses.

At the end of poem, Venus ironically decides to retreat from the world, and to "immure herself, and not be seen" (line 1194). This ending is deeply ironic, since this tendency to self-enclosure makes her something like Adonis. It is also ironic in that we know it is a profoundly temporary situation – she is after all Venus, the goddess of love, and will soon be seeking the next object of her infinite desire. The irony perhaps extends to the pendant poem that Shakespeare was likely contemplating as he finished *Venus and Adonis*. As we shall see in the following chapter, Shakespeare's next published poem will narrate the tragic story of a virtuous woman who unsuccessfully immures herself against a lustful, predatory, tyrannical male. That poem will manifest a very different attitude to lust, placing it in a world where the honor and reputation of a husband and wife are tied up with the wife's impenetrability to any but her husband. Ethical issues that Shakespeare deliberately banishes from *Venus and Adonis* in order to produce a world of near-universal sexual indulgence will come back with a vengeance in that "graver labour." But the accomplishment of that poem should not be allowed to negate the way that Shakespeare in *Venus and Adonis* created a sensual, exuberant world largely untainted by moral judgment. In the first recorded appreciation of Shakespeare, Francis Meres writes in 1598 that "The sweet witty soul of Ovid lives in mellifluous and honey-tongued Shakespeare, witness his Venus and Adonis."[8] The sensual descriptions of the gorgeous bodies and mordant speeches of amorous goddess and reluctant adolescent produce a pleasure that transcends morality, and that has an ecological value all its own.

Chapter 3

Constraint and complaint in *Lucrece*

Short of homicide, rape is the ultimate violation of self.

– Byron R. White

If *Venus and Adonis* features the gorgeous compulsions of pleasure, *Lucrece* turns its attentions to the destructive power of lust.[1] The poem shows in sometimes lugubrious detail how uncontrolled desire destroys both its subject and its object. Fascinated by motive and consequence, the poem is deadly serious in its rigorous exploration of the connections between personal discipline and public government. The final word in the next-to-last line of the poem is "consent," and the poem is designed to explore the connections between political and sexual consent. Political tyranny, the poem suggests, manifests itself most clearly in the predatory and willful action of rape. In fact, Shakespeare includes an "Argument" as an introduction to the poem, to be sure that the reader does not miss the larger trajectory of the story. At the end of the poem, indignation about the rape performed by a member of the royal family leads to the establishment of the Roman republic. As the Argument relates, Brutus offers "a bitter invective against the tyranny of the king: wherewith the people were so moved, that with one consent and a general acclamation the Tarquins were all exiled, and the state government changed from kings to consuls." Rarely has the personal been so closely and overtly allied to the political.[2]

Like *Venus*, the poem is dedicated to the earl of Southampton. The dedication is much warmer, allowing real affection to sift through its conventional deference, as if the relationship between them had developed:

> The love I dedicate to your Lordship is without end; whereof this pamphlet without beginning is but a superfluous moiety. The warrant I have of your honourable disposition, not the worth of my untutored lines, makes it assured of acceptance. What I have done is yours, what

I have to do is yours, being part in all I have devoted yours. Were my worth greater, my duty would show greater; meantime, as it is, it is bound to your Lordship, to whom I wish long life still lengthened with all happiness.

Balancing the "warrant" of Southampton's "honourable disposition" with the "worth of my untutored lines," the dedication attests to a cordial relationship that Shakespeare hopes will continue over the "long life" he wishes to his patron.

The poem fulfills the promise of "some graver labour" which Shakespeare described in the dedication to *Venus*. Like *Venus*, the poem has its source in Ovid, but in this case it is not the *Metamorphoses* but rather the *Fasti*. The story of the famous Roman matron Lucrece had also been told by Livy in the *Historia*, which had been translated into English by William Painter in 1566. The figure of Lucrece had also been mentioned in Chaucer's *Legend of Good Women* (*c.* 1384) and John Gower's *Confessio Amantis* (1390), so Shakespeare would likely have been familiar with the story from a variety of sources. The versions in both Ovid and Livy were common reading in grammar school. Shakespeare's poem, though, is twelve times as long as Ovid's version, and most of the significant additions are in Lucrece's speeches. Shakespeare, it seems, is fascinated by the powerful arguments she musters against her assailant, and by her prolonged analysis of her situation after the rape. Much of the poem is composed of the two extended interior monologues that Lucrece generates as she contemplates the consequences of the rape for herself and her family. In these monologues, the poem participates in the genre of female complaint that was popular at the time.[3]

The two narrative poems share a kind of pendant relationship. *Venus* takes place largely in daytime while *Lucrece* is at night. *Venus* is largely set in the expansive pastoral world of nature, while *Lucrece* takes place in confined interior spaces. John Kerrigan sees the world of *Lucrece* as "claustrophobic" in contrast to the pastoral exuberance of *Venus*.[4] *Lucrece* is almost twice as long as *Venus*. Both poems are composed of stanzas, but in *Venus* Shakespeare used a six-line stanza, while in *Lucrece*, as if to suit his weightier subject, Shakespeare chose a more serious and ambitious vehicle – rhyme royal, which had since Chaucer been the staple of English poetry. Shakespeare would use the stanza again in *A Lover's Complaint*, the long poem published at the end of the 1609 *Shakespeare's Sonnets*, another example of giving voice to a wronged female.

Lucrece was somewhat less popular than *Venus* – eight editions were published before 1640, half the number of editions of *Venus* in the same time frame. Still, *Lucrece* was by most measures a great success. Gabriel Harvey, the sixteenth-century educator and pedant, said that "The younger sort take much delight in Shakespeare's Venus and Adonis," but Lucrece and Hamlet "have it in them to please the wiser sort."[5] By comparison with the lustful comic exuberance of *Venus*, *Lucrece* is solemn, even ponderous. There is none of the gentle humor that enlivens the first poem. It is significant that Harvey mentions *Hamlet* for comparison, since the two works share a focus on motive and consequence rather than action. For all of its verbose speeches, one can see in *Lucrece* the budding dramatist riveted by the capacity of humans to accomplish good and ill, and to justify their choice in interior monologues. In the poem, Shakespeare shows remarkable insight into the mind of a rapist before and after the terrible deed. He also gives us a searing portrait of the physical and emotional damage done to the innocent victim of a terrible crime.

Both poems, of course, are dominated by powerful, intelligent women. It is telling that Shakespeare would choose to inaugurate his career in print by composing two narrative poems centered on women. But where Venus is immortal and in some senses held harmless even for her own predatory sexuality, Lucrece is mortal, extremely vulnerable, and in some ways held responsible for the predatory sexuality of others. Where Venus never consummates her crush on Adonis, Tarquin rapes Lucrece.

Tarquin and predatory lust

The poem begins with "Lust-breathèd Tarquin" (line 3) on his way to Lucrece. We learn that Tarquin "lurks to aspire / And girdle with embracing flames the waist / Of Collatine's fair love, Lucrece the chaste" (lines 5–7). His lust is a "lightless fire" (line 4) that burns and destroys but does not illuminate. It is significant that Shakespeare imagines Tarquin provoked not by the sight of Lucrece but rather by Collatine's report of her virtue. Indeed, in *Lucrece*, Shakespeare is fascinated by the origin and pathology of desire, and seems to implicate the praise offered by a lover in the production of lust in others. In the second and third stanzas of that poem, we are told that Tarquin, the rapist, was initially aroused by Collatine's praise of Lucrece's beauty and chastity:

> Haply that name of "chaste" unhapp'ly set
> This bateless edge on his keen appetite;
> When Collatine unwisely did not let
> To praise the clear unmatchèd red and white
> Which triumphed in that sky of his delight,

Where mortal stars, as bright as heaven's beauties,
With pure aspects did him peculiar duties.

For he the night before, in Tarquin's tent,
Unlocked the treasure of his happy state:
What priceless wealth the heavens had him lent
In the possession of his beauteous mate;
Reck'ning his fortune at such high-proud rate
That kings might be espousèd to more fame,
But king nor peer to such a peerless dame.

(lines 8–21)

Like a sonneteer, Collatine praises the virtue and beauty of his beloved, perhaps partaking of the game in which male status is achieved through proud enumeration of the accomplishments of the spouse. Rome is in this poem revealed to be a world much like Elizabethan England, in which a husband's importance among other men is correlated with his wife's performance of chastity. If so, the process by which Collatine proclaimed his superiority backfires tragically; Collatine's articulation of Lucrece's virtues is what whets the desire that causes him to lose this treasure.

But Shakespeare does not in the least absolve the lustful Tarquin in his emphasis on Collatine's complicity; it is clear that Collatine's praise of Lucrece only "sets the edge" on an already existing appetite, and it is an appetite that Tarquin willfully chooses not to control. Tarquin is proof that, for Shakespeare, happiness does not inhere in the blind satisfaction of desire. Tarquin feels desire, and acts on it, and spreads pain and misery in himself and others in the process. Indeed, he becomes for Shakespeare in his dramatic career a figure paradigmatic for brutal, predatory behavior. Shakespeare returns to the character repeatedly throughout his plays, in *Julius Caesar*, in *Macbeth*, and in *Cymbeline*. In *Julius Caesar*, the reference is largely historical; Brutus, a descendent of the Brutus who speaks at the end of *Lucrece*, remembers that "My ancestors did from the streets of Rome / The Tarquin drive when he was called a king" (2.1.53–54). Macbeth, contemplating the murder of his monarch, sees himself in the figure of Tarquin, one who knowingly acts on his worst impulses:

thus with his stealthy pace,
With Tarquin's ravishing strides, towards his design
Moves like a ghost. (2.1.54–56)

In *Cymbeline*, Giacomo enters Imogen's bedroom concealed in a trunk, and compares his situation to "Tarquin [who] thus / Did softly press the rushes, ere he wakened / The chastity he wounded" (2.2.12–14). Tarquin is for Shakespeare the figure that epitomizes the violent invasion of privacy and the political violation of trust.

The story of Tarquin's rape plays out a central plot in western literature – domestic space is invaded and disturbed by a predatory intruder.[6] In *Lucrece*, though, the rapist is invited into the house, as demanded by the law of hospitality. Shakespeare is particularly interested in the bind that hospitality places on Lucrece. She must welcome her husband's friend, yet there is something implicitly erotic in his presence in the house when her husband is not there. *The Winter's Tale* picks up something of this erotic charge in the eruption of unwarranted jealousy on the part of Leontes at Hermione's success when asking Polixenes to extend his stay. Like Hermione, Lucrece is innocent, yet placed in a situation where her very obedience to men makes her vulnerable to charges of unfaithfulness. When she later remembers her night of terror, Lucrece remarks, as if to the husband whose obligations she thought she fulfilled: "Yet am I guilty of thy honour's wrack; / Yet for thy honour did I entertain him . . . it had been dishonour to disdain him" (lines 841–44). Caught in a web of honor and hospitality, she can do little but invite into the house the very figure who dishonors her. Her innocence, moreover, makes her more vulnerable: as Shakespeare writes, "This earthly saint, adorèd by this devil, / Little suspecteth the false worshipper; / For unstained thoughts do seldom dream on evil" (lines 85–87). Shakespeare is throughout his career fascinated by the way that genuine innocence makes one more susceptible to the treachery of others.

In the poem Shakespeare is far less interested in action than he is in motive and consequence. The rape itself occurs almost before we know it.

> he sets his foot upon the light,
> For light and lust are deadly enemies;
> Shame folded up in blind concealing night,
> When most unseen, then most doth tyrannise.
> The wolf hath seized his prey, the poor lamb cries,
> Till with her own white fleece her voice controlled
> Entombs her outcry in her lips' sweet fold.
>
> For with the nightly linen that she wears
> He pens her piteous clamours in her head,
> Cooling his hot face in the chastest tears
> That ever modest eyes with sorrow shed.
> O that prone lust should stain so pure a bed!
> The spots whereof could weeping purify,
> Her tears should drop on them perpetually.

But she hath lost a dearer thing than life,
And he hath won what he would lose again.
This forcèd league doth force a further strife;
This momentary joy breeds months of pain;

(lines 673–90)

A decidedly unerotic act, the rape is a crime of violence and domination. For Tarquin, perhaps, it offers a "momentary joy," but one that "breeds months of pain." The calculation demonstrates what a bad decision, even from a practical standpoint, he has made. Shakespeare is careful to emphasize Lucrece's superior and continuing chastity – her tears are "chastest," her eyes are "modest" – as if her virtue were a state of mind more than body. But he also acknowledges that Tarquin has "stain[ed] so pure a bed." The crucial question of the poem is whether the stain on the pure bed and the pure woman is nonetheless indelible. We know, for example, that Lady Macbeth's complicity in crime is what makes her unable to remove the imaginary stains of Duncan's blood from her hands. But in *Lucrece* we are led to wonder whether weeping, or any combination of actions, can remove the stain from the innocent victim of a horrible crime, and restore a purity that is defined as a corporeal rather than an ethical condition.

Before the rape, the poem explores the chain of thoughts that lead Tarquin to this despicable action. Shakespeare frames his account of Tarquin's rationalizations with a brief study in the ethics of contentment and self-control, for which Tarquin provides a powerful negative example. Tarquin is seen as one of those insatiable creatures who are "with gain so fond" that "by hoping more they have but less" (lines 134–37). Shakespeare contrasts this perpetual covetousness with a idealized model of contentment: "The aim of all is but to nurse the life / With honour, wealth, and ease in waning age" (lines 141– 42). Yet Shakespeare is always the pragmatist, and he realizes just how hard it is to maintain this sense of contentment, since "in this aim there is such thwarting strife" that we repeatedly must sacrifice one goal for another, "As life for honour in fell battle's rage; / Honour for wealth" (lines 143–46). The "ambitious foul infirmity" that "torments us with defect / Of that we have" makes us "neglect" rather than find satisfaction in "The thing we have" (lines 150–53). The syntax of these passages is sometimes tortured, as if the complex ethical issues required an appropriate form.

But the syntax becomes even more turgid as we observe the self-justifications of Tarquin. For Shakespeare, Tarquin exemplifies the process by which moral values are compromised by covetousness; he makes "Such hazard" by "Pawning his honour to obtain his lust" (lines 155–56). This ethical equivocation produces a deeply divided self, and Shakespeare finds a wonderful syntactical pattern in which to represent that:

> And for himself himself he must forsake
> Then where is truth, if there be no self-trust?
> When shall he think to find a stranger just,
> When he himself himself confounds, betrays
> To sland'rous tongues and wretched hateful days?
>
> (lines 157–61)

The reflexive and repeated "himself himself" shows how Tarquin's lust is leading him to betray his very being and honor. As he leaves his bed, he is a deeply divided creature, "madly tossed between desire and dread" (line 171).

It is fascinating to watch Tarquin's mind at work, distorting and perverting reason to justify an action he knows is wrong. He also knows that the action makes no pragmatic sense:

> What win I if I gain the thing I seek?
> A dream, a breath, a froth of fleeting joy.
> Who buys a minute's mirth to wail a week?
> Or sells eternity to get a toy?
> For one sweet grape who will the vine destroy?
> Or what fond beggar, but to touch the crown,
> Would with the sceptre straight be strucken down?
>
> (lines 211–17)

He also knows that the action he is about to commit is "Shameful," even "Hateful," since it would lead him to betray "my kinsman, my dear friend" (lines 237–40). He is torn between reason and passion, between honor and lust, "'Tween frozen conscience and hot burning will," but his lust wins out: "My will is strong past reason's weak removing" (lines 243–47). In surrendering his passion to will, Tarquin knowingly abdicates the self-rule expected of those in power. "Affection is my captain and he leadeth," Tarquin proclaims with mock-courage; "Desire my pilot is, beauty my prize" (lines 271, 279). It is his internal irresponsibility that ultimately makes him and his clan unworthy of ruling Rome.

Having surrendered to his passion, Tarquin then turns his mind to the perverse project of making "what is vile show like a virtuous deed" (line 252). Tarquin even starts to pray for success, but then realizes the full perversity of that action and pleads compulsion instead: "I must deflower; / The powers to whom I pray abhor this fact" (lines 348–49). He then justifies his action by blaming his future victim. He turns her hospitality back upon her, remembering that "She took me kindly by the hand, / And gazed for tidings in my eager eyes" (lines 253–54). He treats the various locks and doors as inducements to appetite rather than as thresholds he is transgressing. Such hindrances, he says, are "Like little frosts that sometime threat the spring, / To add a more rejoicing to the prime" (lines 331–32). As Lucrece asks for news of "her belovèd Collatinus," Tarquin eroticizes the emotions seen to cross her face:

> O how her fear did make her colour rise!
> First red as roses that on lawn we lay,
> Then white as lawn, the roses took away.
>
> (lines 257–59)

Her expressions of concern for the welfare of her husband are under Tarquin's lustful gaze translated into the amorous palette of red and white that we saw coloring *Venus and Adonis* in the last chapter.

When Lucrece awakes and asks Tarquin what he is doing in her bedroom, he replies:

> The colour in thy face,
> That even for anger makes the lily pale,
> And the red rose blush at her own disgrace,
> Shall plead for me and tell my loving tale.
> Under that colour am I come to scale
> Thy never-conquered fort. The fault is thine,
> For those thine eyes betray thee unto mine.
>
> (lines 477–83)

It is as if he intends to render her responsible for the feelings she has aroused in him. "Thy beauty hath ensnared thee to this night," he declares, completely abdicating responsibility for his actions (line 485). Tarquin tells her that he "must enjoy thee" (line 512), and threatens her with violence and a ruined reputation if she resists:

> If thou deny, then force must work my way;
> For in thy bed I purpose to destroy thee.
> That done, some worthless slave of thine I'll slay,
> To kill thine honour with thy life's decay;
> And in thy dead arms do I mean to place him,
> Swearing I slew him, seeing thee embrace him.
>
> So thy surviving husband shall remain
> The scornful mark of every open eye;
> Thy kinsmen hang their heads at this disdain,

> Thy issue blurred with nameless bastardy:
> And thou, the author of their obloquy,
> Shalt have thy trespass cited up in rhymes,
> And sung by children in succeeding times.
>
> But if thou yield, I rest thy secret friend;
> The fault unknown is as a thought unacted.
>
>   (lines 513–27)

Perversely, he promises to remain her "secret friend" if she will not resist, even as he threatens death to her, and shame to her and her husband, if she resists. This creepy moment provides the fitting culmination of the various relations and trusts he has betrayed.

Lucrece: resistance and complaint

In Ovid, Lucrece remains silent, but Shakespeare creates a profoundly voluble Lucrece who argues at length with Tarquin. Attempting to appeal to his sense of honor and reason, she carefully enumerates the various transgressions he would be committing by raping her. He would be rewarding "hospitality" with "black payment" and he would betray a "friend," her husband. She reminds him that he is "mighty," and that carries responsibilities to a "weakling" such as herself (lines 575–83). She tells him that, as a member of the ruling class, he is obligated to set a good example for his subjects, "For princes are the glass, the school, the book, / Where subjects' eyes do learn, do read, do look" (lines 615–16). She even tries to get him to

> Think but how vile a spectacle it were
> To view thy present trespass in another.
> Men's faults do seldom to themselves appear;
> Their own transgressions partially they smother.
> This guilt would seem death-worthy in thy brother.
>
>   (lines 631–35)

Shakespeare is here perhaps thinking about the power of dramatic illusion to influence behavior by depicting the despicable spectacle and horrible conse-quences of evil deeds. Lucrece appeals finally to the sense of political order that should obtain within Tarquin:

> I sue for exiled majesty's repeal;
> Let him return, and flattering thoughts retire.
> His true respect will prison false desire,

And wipe the dim mist from thy doting eyne,
That thou shalt see thy state, and pity mine.

(lines 640–44)

She tells him further that if he allows his passions, which should be subordinate to reason, to rule his behavior, "So shall these slaves be kind, and thou their slave, / Thou nobly base, they basely dignified" (lines 659–60). It is of course ironic that she pleads for the restoration of the true monarchy of the self within Tarquin, in which sovereign reason would rule over insubordinate passions, since Tarquin's surrender of reason to passion is what will inaugurate the end of the Roman monarchy. Here Shakespeare is exploring the relation between self-rule and the capacity to rule others. He suggests that the proper rule of others is premised on the ability to manage the self. Lucrece is just in the midst of developing further her image of the proper rule of the self when Tarquin passionately interrupts: "'So let thy thoughts, low vassals to thy state'– / 'No more', quoth he. 'By heaven, I will not hear thee! / Yield to my love'" (lines 666–68). The full perversity of his self-deception is announced in his invocation of the terminology of "heaven" and "love."

One can map the attitude to Tarquin's actions by exploring the various images that Shakespeare uses to portray Tarquin's rapacious nature. If her breasts are "ivory globes... A pair of maiden worlds unconquerèd," they become in his imagination like new "worlds" that "in Tarquin new ambition bred" (lines 408–11); he is here like a cruel and rapacious conqueror. A few lines later, he is a "grim lion [who] fawneth o'er his prey" (line 421). He subsequently displays "a cockatrice' dead-killing eye"; the cockatrice was a mythical creature thought to be able to kill simply by its glance. Then he is likened to a "rough beast" who has a "white hind" in his "sharp claws" (lines 540–45). He is also a "foul night-waking cat" who "doth but dally, / While in his hold-fast foot the weak mouse panteth" (lines 554–55). The moment of the rape is marked by the culmination of these images of predation: "The wolf hath seized his prey, the poor lamb cries" (line 677). And our final image of him is less predatory than contemptible: "He like a thievish dog creeps sadly thence" (line 736). Whereas in *Venus and Adonis* animals tend to signify an exuberant reproductive desire shared by all species, in *Lucrece* animals represent the complete repudiation of human kindness or dignity.

Before Tarquin slinks off in disgrace, Shakespeare reminds us of the wretched brevity of his pyrrhic victory: "This momentary joy breeds months of pain; / This hot desire converts to cold disdain" (lines 690–91). We learn that "his soul's fair temple is defacèd"; his passions, which should be "subjects" of the soul, "Have battered down her consecrated wall" and "made her [the soul] thrall / To living death and pain perpetual" (lines 719–26). The oxymorons proliferate in the effort to describe his pathetically confused situation; Tarquin is "A captive victor that hath lost in gain" (line 730). He also suffers from a pathological case of post-coital tristesse:

> Look as the full-fed hound or gorgèd hawk,
> Unapt for tender smell or speedy flight,
> Make slow pursuit, or altogether balk
> The prey wherein by nature they delight,
> So surfeit-taking Tarquin fares this night:
> His taste delicious, in digestion souring,
> Devours his will that lived by foul devouring.
>
> O deeper sin than bottomless conceit
> Can comprehend in still imagination!
> Drunken Desire must vomit his receipt
> Ere he can see his own abomination.
>
> (lines 694–704)

The visceral disgust that suffuses these lines is imagined by Shakespeare to be the inevitable aftermath of indulging unregulated appetite.[7] The predatory imagery that has been hovering around Tarquin throughout the poem comes to rest in the inglorious image of a gluttonous creature made nauseous by surfeiting on the former object of its ravenous appetite.

Tarquin's lengthy and perverse deliberations before the rape are appropriately superseded by Lucrece's immense effort to comprehend and process what has happened to her. The narrator tells us that "she hath lost a dearer thing than life" (line 687). She is left "perplexed in greater pain," and "bears the load of lust he left behind" (lines 733–34). The "load of lust" is both the burden of her victim's guilt and the semen that Tarquin violently forced into her. "Frantic with grief," she laments the dark night that made such subterfuge possible, and at the same time wishes that the night would never end, because "the light will show charactered in my brow / The story of sweet chastity's decay" (lines 762, 807–08). She feels as if the crime she has suffered is stamped on her brow, to be read by all. She knows she is innocent, and yet she also feels sullied by what was done to her against her will. She hopes that her "good name" can "be kept unspotted," yet she also knows that something in which her culture places immense value – the inviolability of the woman in a marriage by any but the husband – has been taken from her by force: "If, Collatine, thine honour lay in me, / From me by strong assault it is bereft" (lines 834–35). Rape was in early modern English law largely defined as a property crime; the word comes from the Latin term for seizure, and originally meant "the act of taking anything by force."[8] But as Shakespeare's Touchstone would say in *As You Like It* (5.4.88), there is "much virtue in 'if.'" The social justice which deems that a husband's honor depends on his wife's impregnabililty – of which neither is in full control – is questioned, albeit briefly and glancingly, in our sense of Lucrece's innocence.

Thrashing about in desperation for things to blame, Lucrece attacks three related abstractions for their cooperation with Tarquin: Night (lines 764–875), Opportunity (lines 876–924), and Time (lines 925–1,022). Then she despairs of the possibility that expressive language – what she calls "This helpless smoke of words" – might be able to address her situation or relieve her agony (line 1,027). She turns to action: "The remedy indeed to do me good / Is to let forth my foul defilèd blood" (lines 1,028–29). She here uses the idea from contemporaneous medicine that disease could be cured by bloodletting to inaugurate her consideration of suicide. The lines also imply a question that will become critical to the poem – is all her blood defiled, or could she, like a Renaissance physician, just let out the defiled blood? Lucrece bestows a purgative power on her own bleeding; she feels that she can "clear this spot by death" (line 1,053).

As she contemplates the degree to which she is tainted by the rape, Lucrece considers the possibility that Tarquin has impregnated her:

> This bastard graff shall never come to growth:
> He shall not boast, who did thy stock pollute,
> That thou art doting father of his fruit.
>
> (lines 1,062–64)

Seeing her value through the eyes of her culture, primarily as the guarantor of Collatine's lineage, Lucrece stumbles upon her own death as the only possible tactic for aborting Tarquin's possible offspring. Indeed, it seems to her to be the only virtuous course of action left. The thought even grants her a brief moment of glorying in her volition, if only in the contemplation of her death: "For me, I am the mistress of my fate" (line 1,069).

Lucrece refuses to participate in the forms of hypocrisy that have victimized her: "My sable ground of sin I will not paint / To hide the truth of this false night's abuses" (lines 1,074–75). She resolves, moreover, to tell her tale, and so to reclaim some of the authority over herself and her story that was stolen in the rape: "My tongue shall utter all" (line 1,076). She hopes that the fervent expression of sorrow might have a purgative function:

> mine eyes, like sluices,
> As from a mountain spring that feeds a dale,
> Shall gush pure streams to purge my impure tale.
>
> (lines 1,076–78)

As tainted as she feels by the crime, she is here able to sort out briefly the purity of her sorrow from the imposed impurity of her story.

Shakespeare terms her a "lamenting Philomel" and in so doing links Lucrece to the proverbial object of rape, a figure from Ovid who was raped and had her tongue cut out by her brother-in-law.[9] Lucrece in fact dislikes the cheerful birdsong that greets the morning because "mirth doth search the bottom of annoy" (line 1,109). Misery, Shakespeare suggests, loves company:

> Sad souls are slain in merry company;
> Grief best is pleased with grief's society;
> True sorrow then is feelingly sufficed
> When with like semblance it is sympathised.
>
> (lines 1,110–13)

Instead of the cheerful morning birds, Lucrece wants to hear the mournful evening song of Philomel, whose situation resembles her own. In this story from Ovid, which seems to have haunted Shakespeare and supplied much of the plot of his early violent tragedy *Titus Andronicus*, Philomel is transformed into the nightingale, whose sad song tells of her victimhood and distress. This is a song that Lucrece could welcome:

> Come Philomel, that sing'st of ravishment,
> Make thy sad grove in my dishevelled hair.
> As the dank earth weeps at thy languishment,
> So I at each sad strain will strain a tear,
> And with deep groans the diapason bear.
>
> (lines 1,128–32)

Lucrece is looking for "co-partners in my pain," because "fellowship in woe doth woe assuage" (lines 789–90).

At the same time, Lucrece wants to hide in solitary darkness because of the intense shame she feels. Shakespeare shows great psychological acuity in his portrait of the suffering and shame experienced by an innocent victim of a horrible crime. Lucrece laments the coming of the daylight, and experiences light not as the promise of a new day but only as a heightened and excruciating visibility. She addresses the sun as the "eye of eyes," and asks it to "Brand not my forehead with thy piercing light" (lines 1,088–91). Lucrece feels as if she is marked by the crime done to her; the very sun whose light might have protected her now becomes the agent of further violation. Later, when she meets one of her servants, she blushes, because "they whose guilt within their bosoms lie / Imagine every eye beholds their blame" (lines 1,342–43). Perhaps the most terrible aspect of the rape is the fact that it occurs in a culture that encourages her to translate into her own "guilt" the horrible act perpetrated by another on her body.

If contemplation of the rape briefly transformed Tarquin into a perverse sophist who uses the structures of ethical philosophy to justify a deeply unethical action, rumination on the consequences of this deed forces Lucrece to confront some of the central questions of western philosophy. Her strategy of abortion by suicide leads her to ask, as Hamlet will later in Shakespeare's career, about the relative virtues of being and not being: "with herself is she in mutiny, / To live or die" (lines 1,153–54). She worries briefly about whether suicide is really a victory over Tarquin or just an extension of Tarquin's violence: "'To kill myself', quoth she, 'alack what were it / But with my body my poor soul's pollution?'" (lines 1,156–57). She imagines her body as the "house" and "temple" of the soul, a temple that is "spotted, spoiled, corrupted, / Grossly engirt with daring infamy" (lines 1,172–73). This imagery allows her to represent her suicide as a way of liberating her "troubled soul" from the "blemished fort" of her body (lines 1,175–76).

It also leads her to imagine suicide not as a further tainting of her soul but rather as a kind of purification ritual. "In my death," she argues, "I murder shameful scorn" (line 1,189). "My blood shall wash the slander of mine ill," Lucrece confidently proclaims (line 1,207). But she will not kill herself until she has identified her rapist to Collatine, and so made clear the reasons for her suicide. When Collatine arrives in response to a letter from Lucrece, Lucrece mounts an explanation and defense which depends on a particular model of body-soul relations. She argues that her essential being is not her body, which has been contaminated by Tarquin, but rather her soul, which remains pure:

> Though my gross blood be stained with this abuse,
> Immaculate and spotless is my mind;
> That was not forced, that never was inclined
> To accessary yieldings, but still pure
> Doth in her poisoned closet yet endure.
>
> (lines 1,655–59)

Her body may be a "poisoned closet," but her mind is "pure," untainted by the crime she has suffered. But the issue is not quite so simple for

Lucrece to dispense with, and quickly evolves into a question rather than a statement:

> What is the quality of mine offence,
> Being constrained with dreadful circumstance?
> May my pure mind with the foul act dispense,
> My low-declinèd honour to advance?
> May any terms acquit me from this chance?
> The poisoned fountain clears itself again;
> And why not I from this compellèd stain?
>
> (lines 1,702–08)

Even when Collatine and the other Roman lords reassure Lucrece that "her body's stain her mind untainted clears," Lucrece chooses to kill herself, naming Tarquin as her rapist and declaring that it is Tarquin in fact who kills her: "He he, fair lords, 'tis he / That guides this hand to give this wound to me" (lines 1,710, 1,721–22). Even in death, the issue of how tainted Lucrece is by the crime remains; the blood from her wound

> doth divide
> In two slow rivers, that the crimson blood
> Circles her body in on every side,
> Who like a late-sack'd island vastly stood
> Bare and unpeopled in this fearful flood.
> Some of her blood still pure and red remained,
> And some looked black, and that false Tarquin stained.
>
> (lines 1,737–43)

The final line has an apt ambiguity; the black blood is both the bodily fluid that Tarquin has stained, and the blood that stains Tarquin, since it identifies him as the rapist, and the ultimate cause of her death.

Shakespeare demonstrates great psychological sympathy and acuity in his portrait of Lucrece, showing how an innocent victim nonetheless feels intense shame, and internalizes the violence done to her. The real tragedy in the poem is not just the horrible crime but the way that Lucrece and her culture define her in terms of what a hypocritical thug has done to her. Lucrece is frequently seen to be proverbial for chastity – Shakespeare works with just this association in *The Taming of the Shrew*, when Petruchio promises Baptista, the father of the shrewish Katherine, that Katherine will prove a "Roman Lucrece for her chastity" (2.1.285). But western commentators have been rather hard on Lucrece. She either gets blamed for her complicity in the rape, or for her suicide. St. Augustine catches her in a double bind, arguing that if Lucrece was in fact not corrupted by Tarquin's rude embraces, then her suicide evinces a damnable despair.[10] Augustine exemplifies the inability of Christianity to sympathize with women who wrestle with the dilemmas into which Christianity repeatedly places them, despite the fact that Lucrece's actions could so easily be mapped onto those of a Christian martyr. It is telling that Shakespeare is little interested in the theological debate on Lucrece's suicide, particularly since that theological debate would ultimately play such a central role in *Hamlet*. Shakespeare instead explores the motivations and the interior spaces of the victim, showing us that the ultimate violation of one's being is not just physical; rather, it is to perpetrate an act which makes the innocent victim feel responsible for it.

Before Collatine and the Romans arrive, Shakespeare provides Lucrece with a moment of precious solace, and in the process meditates on the power of aesthetics to respond to human suffering. When she decides to tell Collatine in person rather than by letter, she theorizes about the respective power of narrative and spectacle:

> To see sad sights moves more than hear them told,
> For then eye interprets to the ear
> The heavy motion that it doth behold,
> When every part a part of woe doth bear.
> 'Tis but a part of sorrow that we hear:
> Deep sounds make lesser noise than shallow fords,
> And sorrow ebbs, being blown with wind of words.
>
> (lines 1,324–30)

When the despondent Lucrece subsequently gazes at a painting of the sack of Troy, she looks for a face "where all distress is stelled" (line 1,444), and finds it in the figure of "despairing Hecuba":

> In her the painter had anatomised
> Time's ruin, beauty's rack, and grim care's reign;
> Her cheeks with chops and wrinkles were disguised;
> Of what she was no semblance did remain.
> Her blue blood changed to black in every vein,
>   Wanting the spring that those shrunk pipes had fed,
> Showed life imprisoned in a body dead.   (lines 1,450–56)

Hecuba of course is a figure to whom Shakespeare would return in *Hamlet*.[11] Lucrece finds in her a figure whose emotional agony is commensurate with her own. Shakespeare explores the painter's capacity to find physical correlatives for the devastations of immense internal suffering, and investigating in the process the potentially salutary effects of viewing another's agony.

Lucrece, we learn, finds a particular model of emotional self-fashioning in Hecuba's grief:

> On this sad shadow Lucrece spends her eyes,
> And shapes her sorrow to the beldam's woes,
>   (lines 1457–58)

As "feelingly she weeps Troy's painted woes" (line 1492), Lucrece completely loses track of the time, or of her own tragic situation. Shakespeare here is interested in the idea that aesthetic absorption can have temporary soothing effects for afflicted souls.

Lucrece in fact is transported from her tragic situation by her commiserative encounter with the painting:

> Which all this time hath overslipped her thought
> That she with painted images hath spent,
> Being from the feeling of her own grief brought
> By deep surmise of others' detriment,
> Losing her woes in shows of discontent.
>   It easeth some, though none it ever curèd,
>   To think their dolour others have endurèd.
>   (lines 1,576–82)

Through sympathetic identification with another's suffering, Shakespeare suggests, Lucrece discovers some temporary relief from her fierce pain. A classic example of *ekphrasis*, the literary description of a work of visual art, the passage allows Shakespeare to reflect on his practice and function of writing violent dramas depicting immense agony. As Lucrece ruminates on the fall of Troy, we can see Shakespeare ruminating on the possible affect and use of such spectacles of suffering.

Founding the Roman republic

The poem, though, ends not with aesthetic rumination on the power of spectacle but rather with political action. Almost comically, Lucrece's husband and her father argue over who experiences the greater loss with her death:

> Then son and father weep with equal strife
> Who should weep most, for daughter or for wife.

> The one doth call her his, the other his;
> Yet neither may possess the claim they lay.

> The father says "She's mine." "O, mine she is",
> Replies her husband.   (lines 1,791–96)

Shakespeare seems to find the capacity of patriarchy to produce a dispute over the body of a woman to be inappropriate and even silly. As the two males to whom Lucrece owed allegiance selfishly battle over their loss, a figure named Brutus, who had pretended to be a fool as a strategy of survival in a treacherous court, turns Lucrece into a cause célèbre for the Roman republic. Brutus taps into the powerful emotions aroused by the spectacle of Lucrece's death, and offers a rousing speech, vowing that "We will revenge the death of this true wife" (line 1,841). Lucrece's story and bleeding body then become props in the banishment of Tarquin, and the beginning of the Roman republic:

> They did conclude to bear dead Lucrece thence,
> To show her bleeding body thorough Rome,
> And so to publish Tarquin's foul offence;
> Which being done with speedy diligence,
> The Romans plausibly did give consent
> To Tarquin's everlasting banishment.
>   (lines 1,850–55)

The ending of the poem is less politically oriented than the Argument that prefaces the poem. In the Argument, Shakespeare spells out the precise political meanings of this banishment:

> bearing the dead body to Rome, Brutus acquainted the people with the doer and manner of the vile deed, with a bitter invective against the tyranny of the king: wherewith the people were so moved, that with one consent and a general acclamation the Tarquins were all exiled, and the state government changed from kings to consuls.

At the end of the poem, by contrast, he chooses to emphasize the personal revenge for Lucrece's rape rather than its explicitly political dimensions. Still, the word that ends the next-to-last line of the poem – "consent" – cleverly unites the political and the personal dimensions of the poem. Tyranny is government without consent, and rape is sex without consent.[12]

In some ways, *Venus and Adonis* and *Lucrece* tell the same story in very different keys. Both poems explore the intersection of eroticism and power by focusing on a circumstance when desire is not mutual. Where *Venus* finds comedy and sensuality in the scenario of the goddess of love unsuccessfully seducing an adolescent male, *Lucrece* discovers relentless tragedy in the predatory actions of a lustful male. Both poems are dominated by compelling women, whose exuberant lust or oppressive misery is explored at great length. In *Venus*,

Adonis is turned into a flower which Venus plucks and holds to her breast, while in *Lucrece*, the matron's body becomes a stage property in male plays for power. *Lucrece* is, finally, a poem which uses the analogy between male power over the female body and inherited power in the state to articulate the abuses of position. Shakespeare will write a sonnet about those "that have pow'r to hurt, and will do none" (Sonnet 94).[13] *Lucrece* is in part a poem about one who has power to hurt, and chooses to do so. It is also about the hurt that person inflicts. In its lengthy exploration of Tarquin's perverse motives and Lucrece's devout misery, the poem hones Shakespeare's growing fascination with motive and emotion. This fascination helps produce the magnificent plays; it is also what drives the Sonnets, which will be the subject of the next three chapters.

Chapter 4

Mysteries of the Sonnets

Dedication, publication, sequence, characters

> There has been more nonsense written about Shakespeare's Sonnets than about any other piece of literature extant.
>
> – W. H. Auden

There are few texts for which it would not be overkill to devote an entire chapter to what we do not know. But the Sonnets have been so obscured by clouds of speculation that it seems important to clear the air by saying what we know and don't know about them before we start reading them. Interpretation of the Sonnets is frequently interwoven with a series of seductive possibilities and undemonstrable hypotheses. When so little is certain, it is best to confess the limits of our knowledge, and begin to work from there.

Publication and dedication

The Sonnets were first published in 1609, in a volume entitled *Shake-Speares Sonnets. Never before Imprinted.* But even this claim is at best a half-truth. In 1599, versions of two sonnets (ones that become Sonnets 138 and 144) were published in a volume entitled *The Passionate Pilgrim*, a small collection of twenty poems purporting to be by Shakespeare. Only five of the poems are known to be by Shakespeare – the two sonnets, and versions of three sonnets from Shakespeare's play *Love's Labour's Lost*. The volume was apparently designed to exploit Shakespeare's growing reputation as a dramatist and as a non-dramatic poet; the title may be a reference to a line in the popular *Romeo and Juliet*, where lips are imagined as "two blushing pilgrims." Several of the poems in *The Passionate Pilgrim* that are not by Shakespeare deal with the theme of Venus and Adonis, the subject of Shakespeare's extremely popular narrative poem. We don't know how the publisher, William Jaggard, came to possess the two sonnets, although it is likely some manuscript was made available to him. We also don't know whether the differences between the two Shakespearean sonnets he publishes and the version published in 1609 are a result of authorial revision or textual corruption. If it is authorial revision, we are not sure which is the revised version.

Shake-Speares Sonnets was published by Thomas Thorpe. It is likely that Shakespeare participated in some form in the publication of this volume; at the very least, he did not dispute it (which would be surprising for one so litigious in matters of real estate and money owed).[1] But the dedication is not by Shakespeare – rather it is by "T. T.," whom we have assumed is the publisher Thorpe, in part because publishers would sometimes compose the dedications to volumes they published, and in part because no other candidates with the right initials have been suggested. This dedication is one of the more enigmatic utterances in all of western literature.

TO THE ONLIE BEGETTER OF
THESE INSUING SONNETS
MR. W. H. ALL HAPPINESSE
AND THAT ETERNITIE
PROMISED
BY
OUR EVER-LIVING POET
WISHETH
THE WELL-WISHING
ADVENTURER IN
SETTING
FORTH
T. T.

We are not sure why Thorpe rather than Shakespeare wrote the dedication, but it does suggest that Shakespeare was not closely involved with the volume. In *Venus and Adonis* and *Lucrece*, as we have seen, Shakespeare took great care over the composition of the dedication. If Shakespeare were actively involved in preparing the sonnets for publication, he would likely have written the dedication. It is also likely that he would have given the collection a different title, since collections of sonnets regularly had witty titles such as *Astrophil and Stella* (translated as "star-lover and star"). *Shake-Speares Sonnets* does not sound like the title a conventional early modern author would choose to present his work to the world. But one of the most striking things about the collection is its cultivated unconventionality.

We don't know who "Mr. W. H." is. It could refer to Henry Wriothesley, the earl of Southampton, to whom Shakespeare had already dedicated *Venus and Adonis* and *Lucrece*. This would require a dyslexic transposition of the "W." and the "H." by the printer, and a failure to recognize the earl's exalted position by using the less deferential "Mr." Some of the early sonnets encouraging a beautiful young man to procreate sound a lot like Venus' efforts to seduce Adonis; we do know that Wriothesley was reluctant to get married. Another strong candidate is William Herbert, the third earl of Pembroke; Herbert would later be one of the two dedicatees of the First Folio of Shakespeare's collected dramatic works in 1623. And the initials are at least in the right order. But, again, "Mr." is a brazenly inappropriate way to address an earl, particularly in a dedication, a genre which frequently elicited exaggerated deference. It is possible that the addressee of the 1609 Sonnets is deliberately left obscure, to entice speculation, and so help sales.[2] If so, it certainly succeeded in the long run by eliciting mountains of conjecture, but in the short run it did not help much with sales. The sonnets were not reprinted until 1640, and then in a radically different edition.

We are not sure what the phrase "ONLIE BEGETTER" means in the dedication. Typically, in dedicatory situations, the fiction obtains that the patron has through nurturing the artist functioned as a kind of creator, and now has a proprietary claim on the work. That may be at work here. Shakespeare uses a version of this trope in the dedication of *Lucrece* to Southampton when he declares that "What I have done is yours." The phrase "ONLIE BEGETTER" could, then, refer to a patron. Just as easily, it could refer to the person who inspired the poems, and who was the object of their ardent devotion. The person would "beget" the poems by creating the circumstances for the emotions that they record. And, of course, it could refer to the actual composition of the poems, since the relationship between poet and poetry is frequently figured as that between a parent and child.[3] It is perhaps significant that Thorpe chooses this procreative metaphor, since the early sonnets are involved in the effort to convince a beautiful young man to procreate.

Thorpe, the probable author of the dedication (no other candidates for "T. T." have been proposed), seems to have read at least some of the early poems attentively. When he suggests that "Mr. W. H." will merit "THAT ETERNITIE PROMISED BY OUR EVER-LIVING POET," Thorpe is certainly picking up on the way that many of the poems grapple with the ravages of time, and hope to bestow eternal fame on the beloved. (This thematic cluster will be the subject of the next chapter.) Thorpe also suggests here that poetry may not just be a way for the poet to commemorate another human for eternity, as Shakespeare repeatedly writes, but rather a way for the poet to become "ever-living." Indeed, one of the many ironies suffusing the publication is that we do not know who any of the figures are to whom Shakespeare promises eternity, but we certainly know the poet, whose own fame and reputation survives in just the way he hopes to bestow it on the objects of his poetry.

We cannot be sure when Shakespeare wrote the poems. Obviously, by 1599 there were drafts available of the two sonnets that were published in *The Passionate Pilgrim*. Also, in 1598, a clergyman named Francis Meres offers a significant mention of Shakespeare in a published commonplace book called *Palladis Tamia: Wits Treasury*. In a section designed to compare "our English Poets, with the Greek, Latin, and Italian Poets," Meres praises Shakespeare as the poet of *Venus and Adonis* and *Lucrece*, his two highly successful published poems, but also offers the first mention of Shakespeare's unpublished work in sonnets:

> The sweet wittie soule of Ovid lives in mellifluous & hony-tongued *Shakespeare*, witness his *Venus* and *Adonis*, his *Lucrece*, his sugred Sonnets among his private friends, &c.[4]

It is likely, then, that at least some sonnets were circulating in manuscript well before 1609. Sonnet 2 in particular shows up in a lot of manuscripts from the period. The adjective "sugred" may provide a clue, but the two poems published in *The Passionate Pilgrim* – Sonnets 138 and 144 – are not poems to which one would be tempted to apply that adjective, since they are two of the most cynical sonnets Shakespeare ever wrote. Some scholars have employed stylometric analyses using vocabulary and syntax from the plays (since their dates of composition are better known) to determine when clusters of sonnets were written. These studies have proven suggestive, but unpersuasive and inconclusive.[5] Such analysis is still a blunt instrument at best, particularly when the data set is not larger.

The temptations of autobiography and sequence

Unlike most previous sonneteers, Shakespeare does not give names to the characters that populate his sonnets. There is nothing like Sidney's Stella or Spenser's Elizabeth. But Shakespeare does refer to his own first name more frequently than most sonneteers, particularly in a group of later sonnets which develop puns on the poet's name – "Will" – and his desire, or "will." Also, in Sonnet 145 most critics hear a pun on the last name of the woman Shakespeare married, Anne Hathaway, in "hate away" in line 13:

Those lips that Love's own hand did make
Breathed forth the sound that said "I hate"
To me that languish'd for her sake;
But when she saw my woeful state,
Straight in her heart did mercy come,
Chiding that tongue that ever sweet
Was used in giving gentle doom,
And taught it thus anew to greet:
"I hate" she alter'd with an end,
That follow'd it as gentle day
Doth follow night, who like a fiend
From heaven to hell is flown away;
"I hate" from hate away she threw,
And saved my life, saying "not you."

The poem's comparatively unsophisticated tetrameter and simplistic plot also leads most critics to think this was one of the first sonnets Shakespeare composed. It certainly feels out of place amid a series of poems dedicated to scouring the darkest aspects of jealousy, infidelity, and desire. Nonetheless, its riddling mention of Shakespeare's wife's name does affiliate it with those poems that turn on the various meanings of Shakespeare's first name, "Will."

We do not know how autobiographical the poems are. Sonnet 145 sounds as if it could have emerged from a real-life courtship situation, but this may be completely misleading, or a verbal *trompe l'oeil* created by a clever artist. Sonnets 135, 136, and 143 pun repeatedly on the name "Will," and are enhanced by our knowledge that "Will" is the first name of the author. But they are more interested in exploring the kaleidoscope of meanings available in the word "will" than in revealing biographical circumstances or innermost thoughts of the author. Some poems refer to a rival poet (76–86, and 100–03); the poet mentions a rival for the patronage and affection of a young man, and experiences jealousy of his rival's "worthier pen" and "better spirit." But we do not know whether these poems refer to a real rivalry, a general sense of a competitive literary marketplace, or a completely fictional scenario that serves the poet's goals of exploring the various faces of jealousy in verse. Even if real, the poems could designate a single figure or a composite of various writers in a competitive marketplace.[6]

We don't know whether the Sonnets offer a window on Shakespeare's sexual identity, or are simply evidence of his remarkable ability to ventriloquize convincingly a range of erotic scenarios and desires. It is tempting to side with Stephen Booth's clever summary of the issue: "William Shakespeare was almost certainly homosexual, bisexual, or heterosexual. The sonnets provide no evidence on the matter."[7] Certainly the emotions articulated in many of the poems feel authentic. But this may just be a measure of the poet's art. In 1593, at the time that Shakespeare was likely composing some of the sonnets, Giles Fletcher the Elder wisely suggested that there was no necessary connection between the subject of a poem and the life of an author: "a man may write of love, and not be in love, as well as of husbandrie, and not goe to plough: or of witches, and be none: or of holinesse, and be flat prophane."[8] No one to my knowledge has claimed that Shakespeare was a murderer despite his remarkable ability to imagine the interior feelings of one in *Macbeth*. Scholars and readers have been divided between viewing the Sonnets as proto-Romantic autobiographical confession and as a random set of mere literary exercises. William Wordsworth, the Romantic poet *par excellence*, famously suggested of the Sonnets that "with this key, / Shakespeare unlocked his heart." Robert Browning, the leading Victorian practitioner of the dramatic monologue, responded: "If so, the less Shakespeare he."[9] Wordsworth's comment certainly gets at something the poems appear to offer – a kind of inner confessional monologue. Yet, as Browning's comment reminds us, the poems are not heart-rending confessions, or even the "spontaneous overflow of powerful emotion remembered in tranquillity," but rather artful utterances carefully designed to look like impassioned confession.[10] The Sonnets are tantalizing because they seem to be our only chance to hear Shakespeare, the consummate dramatist, speak with something like his own voice. But we need to remember that Shakespeare's greatest dramatic innovation was probably the soliloquy, the deliberate staging of inner dialogue to sound like thought. It should be no surprise that Shakespeare's poetry would also exhibit the compelling illusion of the articulate expression of the deepest thoughts and feelings.

We certainly don't know whether Shakespeare intended the 154 sonnets he wrote to be read as a sequence. Certainly groups of poems talk to each other; throughout the collection, moreover, poems tend to cluster around certain themes. This tendency to coagulate around certain recurring motifs will be the organizational principle of the next two chapters on the Sonnets. In these chapters, I will discuss the Sonnets as clusters of discrete but overlapping themes. We will never know for sure whether Shakespeare assigned the poems the numbers that they exhibit in the 1609 edition, but this has not prevented many scholars from using Renaissance numerology to assign meaning to these numbers.[11] We should be willing to consider the possibility that Thorpe collected scattered sonnets written for various audiences, purposes, and occasions, and then engaged in his own act of creative re-presentation. This phenomenon of creative compiling was common in the manuscript and publishing cultures of the period.

One of the joys and challenges of reading the collection is attending to the various patterns that do emerge, whether or not Shakespeare intended them. The collection, first of all, has traditionally been divided into two large sequences: Sonnets 1–126, most of which are written to a beautiful young man (although many of these poems do not specify the sex of the addressee, and we must be careful not to presume too much from context and sequence); and Sonnets 127–52, which are written to or about a "dark lady." In addition, there are many small thematic clusters and narrative sequences scattered throughout the collection. Sonnets 1–17, for example, urge a beautiful young man to reproduce; along the way, they inaugurate a recurring meditation on poetry as a mode of reproduction and an avenue to immortality. Sonnets 27–28 and 43 are concerned with insomnia, and suggest that anxiety about the beloved is the cause of the inability to rest. Sonnets 33–35 and 41–42 depict some kind of erotic betrayal on the part of the beloved. Sonnets 36–39 and 43–47 recount the friend's physical absence, and the speaker's efforts to comfort himself amid the emotional pain of separation. Sonnets 78–90 describe a rival poet and lover, in which literary patronage and erotic relations are blurred. Sonnets 91–96 seem to tell a story, where the poet and the Young Man quarrel and then reconcile, perhaps after some erotic betrayal on the part of the Young Man. In Sonnets 100–20 the poet apologizes for his apparent inability to be constant to the Young Man, although it is unclear if his infidelity is sexual or literary. Sonnet 126 has only twelve lines, and seems to signal a major transition in the collection. Sonnets 127, 128, and 130 bestow compliments on a woman whose attractions belie standard definitions linking beauty with a fair complexion. Sonnets 133–34 suggest that the lady has been repeatedly unfaithful, perhaps even with the Young Man of the first 126 sonnets. As mentioned above, Sonnets 135, 136, and 143 develop puns on the poet's name – "Will" – and his desire, or "will." Sonnets 153 and 154, the last sonnets in the collection, are poems on the power of Cupid, and depict the futility of human efforts to "cure" the disease of love.

The temptation to transform these clusters into a kind of coherent narrative is great.[12] The collection as it comes down to us conspires with our craving for narrative continuity to create an appetite for coherence, an appetite the collection whets but cannot sate. Far more diffuse and disconnected than the sonnet sequences composed by Shakespeare's contemporaries, the collection nonetheless stirs the same generic expectations. Like a flipbook with many pages missing, the collection seems to ask us to supply a story that would tell us what has happened between the poems. Readers want to reorganize the poems, to dramatize them, to imagine them as episodes in an evolving story. In the chapters that follow, we will not totally resist this temptation – if we did, we would lose such handy and hallowed signifiers as "Dark Lady" and "Young Man." But we will try to remain fully aware when we are succumbing to the temptation, and to mark it as such. When reading the Sonnets, we will make every effort to acknowledge the inevitable tension that arises between the integrity of an individual poem and the narrative and thematic contexts which surround it. We will also try to make the integrity of the individual poem a paramount concern, since individual sonnets are the only things that we can be reasonably sure are the product of Shakespeare's intention. We will, furthermore, take comfort in the knowledge that there are no significant disputes about the authorship of any of the sonnets in the collection. A remarkable study in the seductive allure of inference and innuendo, the 1609 Sonnets at once whet and frustrate our longings for autobiographical correlatives, narrative shape, and aesthetic closure. An important part of reading them is separating out what they do give us from what we wish they gave us.

Characters and reception

Because Shakespeare does not bestow names on the characters to which his sonnets refer, as contemporaneous sonneteers so frequently did, subsequent readers and critics have more than made up the difference. The central characters have acquired weirdly allegorical names from which we infer archetypal roles that belie their individual complexity: the Young Man, the Rival Poet, and the Dark Lady. It is possible that all three are illusions produced by readers in search of fantasies of narrative continuity. It is also possible that all three figures are mere literary inventions, "airy nothings" like Caliban or Ariel on which Shakespeare bestowed a "local habitation and a name."[13] It is also possible that all three are specific historical characters with whom Shakespeare had relations of one sort or another, about which we will never know. Many scholars have assumed that there are real correlatives for these figures in Shakespeare's life, and numerous candidates have been proposed for them, with varying degrees of persuasion and ingenuity. As we read the Sonnets, we need to remember that the Young Man, the Rival Poet, and the Dark Lady are critical fictions; but we also need to remember that they are fictions at least partially produced by the poems themselves.

We are not even sure what a descriptive term like darkness means when referring to the Dark Lady.[14] At times, it seems her darkness is simply a literary darkness, a convention that encourages the productions of poems in praise of brown beauty as a test of the poet's ability to praise successfully one who defies standard conventions of beauty located in a "fair," that is light, complexion. Sonnet 130, "My mistress' eyes," certainly participates in this tradition. Yet, at other moments, the darkness of the Dark Lady is more ethical than epidermal; it is a sign of her promiscuity and infidelity. There are even passages in which her darkness seems as if it is linked to contemporary notions of race.

We cannot be certain that Shakespeare wrote *A Lover's Complaint*, the poem appended to the 1609 Sonnets. The poem is attributed to him, but such attributions are frequently faulty particularly when dealing with a popular poet such as Shakespeare, whose literary reputation and economic clout had already been exploited by the compiler of *The Passionate Pilgrim*. We also don't know whether Shakespeare intended the poem to be published at the end of the Sonnets, if he indeed wrote it. *A Lover's Complaint* might be a fugitive poem seized by a rogue publisher to fill out the 1609 volume, or it might be Shakespeare's own deliberate conclusion to the Sonnets. John Kerrigan has made perhaps our most eloquent defense of the poem being Shakespeare's, arguing that this "beautiful and neglected poem" provides a powerful coda to the stories of love fulfilled or betrayed in the Sonnets. Brian Vickers, on the other hand, has recently produced a vigorous attack on the idea of Shakespeare's authorship, basing his argument largely on a combination of aesthetic judgment and stylometric analysis.[15] In this book, I operate under the assumption that the poem is indeed by Shakespeare, and is thematically connected to the Sonnets with which it is published.

We know almost nothing about Shakespeare's process of composing the Sonnets. We do, though, have a fascinating account of Shakespeare's process of composing drama, as witnessed by the compilers of the First Folio, John Heminges and Henry Condell. They offer a fascinating account of Shakespeare's almost unbelievable fluency, at least when he was writing plays: "what he thought, he uttered with that easiness, that we have scarce received from him a blot in his papers." This account is supported by Ben Jonson's envious lament: "I remember the players have often mentioned it as an honor to Shakespeare that in his writing, whatever he penned, he never blotted out a line. My answer hath been, 'Would he had blotted a thousand.'"[16] It may, however, be telling that in *Lucrece* we glimpse a somewhat different creative process, which may reflect the processes of composing formally patterned poetry. When Lucrece decides to write a letter to Collatine, she experiences some interesting pangs of composition that may represent the painstaking effort required of even a Shakespeare to write stanzaic poetry:

> Conceit and grief an eager combat fight:
> What wit sets down is blotted straight with will.
> This is too curious good; this blunt and ill.
>
> (lines 1,298–1,300)

While it seems that part of her creative problem is the strong emotion she is experiencing, the reasons for blotting quickly become aesthetic: "too curious good," "blunt and ill." This is certainly the scenario, otherwise gratuitous, of someone who knows what it is to struggle with writing. It is possible that Shakespeare offers here via the figure of Lucrece a glimpse of the process of agonized self-censorship required to write what *A Lover's Complaint* aptly calls "deep-brained sonnets." The tension experienced by Lucrece between "wit" and "will," between form and content, between idea and emotion, remains highly productive throughout the Sonnets.

Probably because of a human longing for teleological narratives, critics tend to exaggerate the differences between the first 126 poems and the last 28. They translate sequence into consequence, and inject narratives of increasing intricacy into the change of love objects from a beautiful young man to a dark lady. Underpinning the claims for the developing psychological and aesthetic complexity of the collection is a curious, even inverted sense of time in the sequence as it comes down to us – the "early" (lower-numbered) poems explicitly refer to the poet's age, and frequently contrast his advanced age with the Young Man's youth. But the "later" (higher-numbered) poems seem to invoke more of a sense of love among chronological equals; at least, the poems don't seem to need to address the issue of age difference as frequently as the "early" poems do. Both segments deal with issues of sexual betrayal and spiritual infidelity. Both segments deal with rivals and love triangles. Both segments confront the psychological division involved in loving an object that does not live up to one's ideals. Indeed, the most overtly religious poem in the collection is buried amid the so-called Dark Lady sonnets – Sonnet 146.

Unlike *Venus* and *Lucrece*, the Sonnets did not receive much acclaim for the first 150 years after publication; despite Shakespeare's fame, thirty-one years would pass before the second edition. This may have been in part because of timing: by the time they were published, the fad for sonnet sequences had disappeared. When they were published in 1640, it was in a very different format and order. In a volume entitled *POEMS: VVRITTEN BY WIL. SHAKESSPEARE. Gent.*, John Benson reordered and combined various poems. Perhaps aspiring to produce the poetic equivalent of the First Folio, Benson also included an engraved portrait of Shakespeare and a range of commendatory poems by John Milton (reprinted from the Second Folio [1630]), Ben Jonson, Francis Beaumont, Robert Herrick and others. The text combines most of Shakespeare's sonnets with poems from *The Passionate Pilgrim*, and also contains *A Lover's Complaint*, and "The Phoenix and Turtle." The edition notoriously changes three masculine pronouns to feminine, and includes titles that would lead a reader to assume that most of the poems apparently written to a young man in the 1609 volume were actually to a woman. For the next 150 years, Benson's edition was the "authoritative" edition of Shakespeare's poetry. It was not until 1790 that the great editor Edmond Malone restored the 1609 edition to the primacy we still assume it merits.[17]

A final mystery of the Sonnets worth noting is their radical departure from the conventions of the standard sonnet sequence. Shakespeare's Sonnets aggressively alter and expand the range of available subjects for sonnets, and sonnet collections. Rather than the conventional plot of a male courting a distant female, in Shakespeare's Sonnets we get the following profoundly unconventional scenarios: sonnets urging a beloved young man to procreate in order to preserve his beauty (1–17); a poem about how the Young Man was first a woman until a feminized Nature "pricked him out" (20); a sonnet equivocally praising the merits of stony self-control (94); a sonnet filled with disgust at the ethics and mechanics of orgasm (129); and a sonnet where love is a disease spread in a love triangle (144). It is unusual, moreover, for a collection of sonnets to switch addressee three-quarters of the way through. This could be an argument either for the randomness of the collection, or for Shakespeare's formal innovation, in describing how one type of relationship mirrors, or is replaced by, another. One aspect of the sonnet sequence that may have attracted Shakespeare is its capacity to represent formally a conclusion which is at once provisional and profound. If Shakespeare's dramaturgy is marked by a growing skepticism about the possibility of comprehensive answers, it is hard to imagine a more attractive format in non-dramatic poetry than the sonnet sequence, which offers both the pleasure of temporary closure, and the contingency of all conclusions.

In part about desire and the desire for knowledge, the Sonnets tantalize readers with possibilities of half-known or partially insinuated biographical information. Entering the world in a publication that may or may not be authorized, the Sonnets have always seemed to conceal as much as they reveal. They profess ardent affection for mobile, transient, and largely inscrutable objects of erotic attraction. Meres also praises Shakespeare as one of "the most passionate among us to bewaile and bemoane the perplexities of Love." Because of reasons and circumstances we will never know, the Sonnets express the terrors and pleasures of emotional attachment with unprecedented vigor and precision. I would argue that the phenomenon of Shakespeare's so-called "invention of lyric subjectivity" is chimerical, but at the same time completely understandable as a response to the compelling phantoms of interiority that the poems conjure.[18]

Hamlet tells Rosencrantz and Guildenstern in exasperation that "You would play upon me, you would seem to know my stops, you would pluck out the heart of my mystery" (3.2.335–36). The following two chapters, dedicated to different thematic streams that course through the Sonnets, do not try to pluck out the heart of the volume's myriad mysteries; rather, these chapters aspire to acknowledge Shakespeare's efforts to find a language and form that would encapsulate the extremities of love. Filled with accidental and willed mysteries, Shakespeare's Sonnets investigate the feverish horrors of giving in to love, and the chilling nausea of remaining indifferent to its pleasures; they dwell on the distressing transience of existence, and argue that this transience at once makes things more valuable and drains them of meaning. The Sonnets carefully explore the relations and distinctions between erotic and emotional desire; in both the poems to a beautiful young man and those written about a dark lady, Shakespeare painstakingly records the mostly unsuccessful effort to synchronize these two forms of longing. Eloquently transcribing the aspiration of human love to eternity, the Sonnets nonetheless reveal these aspirations to be ultimately unsatisfying, and directed from changeable and transient beings toward changeable and transient beings. One of the most powerful documents of the vagaries and possibilities of human desire that we possess, the Sonnets plumb the exalted promises and elusive mysteries of human erotic attachment in all its forms. For all of the mysteries that surround them, the Sonnets themselves sound the deepest mysteries of human commitment.

Chapter 5

Time and mortality in the Sonnets

Tombs die too.

– Roland Barthes

The ruination of time is not a subject unique to poetry. Indeed, one of the central themes of love poetry – *carpe diem*, seize the day, for tomorrow we die – derives its energy and persuasiveness from the inevitable passing of youth. But Shakespeare's particular angle on time and its relationship to poetry and desire must have struck the first readers of the Sonnets as an odd, if not a radical, variation on a conventional theme. Time is an important if intermittent issue in the first 126 sonnets. The word itself is mentioned 78 times. But with one notable exception, it is hardly present at all as a theme or issue in the last 28 poems. Time is for Shakespeare rarely imagined as healing or redemptive (although the late romances, and *The Winter's Tale* in particular, will engage with the possibility that intense suffering over substantial chunks of time might merit some qualified forgiveness for truly horrible acts). Rather, time in the Sonnets is a force that ravages beauty and destroys objects of love and desire. It even threatens the immaterial substance of memory, which is precariously lodged in the heart and brain of creatures whose fragile bodies are subject to temporal dissolution.

Time and progeny

The first nineteen sonnets focus on the precarious and ephemeral beauty of an aristocratic young man, and worry about the toll that time will take on his physical charms. In the first sonnet, the speaker assumes that everything decays, and uses praise of a young man's beauty to urge him to reproduce, and so to preserve his beauty through progeny:

> From fairest creatures we desire increase,
> That thereby beauty's rose might never die,
> But as the riper should by time decease,
> His tender heir might bear his memory:
> But thou, contracted to thine own bright eyes,
> Feed'st thy light's flame with self-substantial fuel,
> Making a famine where abundance lies,
> Thyself thy foe, to thy sweet self too cruel.
> Thou that art now the world's fresh ornament
> And only herald to the gaudy spring,
> Within thine own bud buriest thy content
> And, tender churl, makest waste in niggarding.
> Pity the world, or else this glutton be,
> To eat the world's due, by the grave and thee.

The opening line signals to the reader that these poems inhabit a territory very different from conventional sonnet sequences. This is not the anticipated love poem to a distant female beloved, but rather an utterance between men. Articulating a theory of aesthetics and of sexual selection, the speaker suggests that beautiful males choose attractive females because they produce more attractive progeny. The phrase "fairest creatures," which would typically refer to women, applies here to both beautiful males like the Young Man and to the beings with whom he is urged to mate. Women are valued for their procreative powers; they are the creatures who enable the further reproduction of beautiful males, and they do a better job of this when they themselves are beautiful. The responsibility of a beautiful male aristocrat, the poem argues, is to occasion the further proliferation of beauty. The poem criticizes the Young Man for being too self-enclosed and self-involved. This is a strange and interesting spin on the traditional *carpe diem*; the Young Man is being urged to have sex with someone who is not the speaker in order to convey an image of his beauty into the future. The poem suggests that if the Young Man would only reproduce a "tender heir" to "bear his memory," he would offer a provisional defeat of the inevitable "grave." The final appeal in the couplet resembles gestures in conventional love poetry; where the standard lover would appeal to the "pity" of his beloved, the speaker of Sonnet 1 asks a young man to "pity the world" by reproducing.

This appeal to procreation as a way of defeating time may seem to us a bit odd. But this was a culture that was far more likely than we are to imagine the essential self as defined by its place in a lineage and kinship network. Indeed, as John Hayward argues in 1603, a time when Shakespeare may well have been composing some sonnets, "the Succession of Children is one of the primary precepts of nature: whereby his mortality is in some sort repaired, and continuance perpetuated by his posterity."[1] By urging the Young Man to reproduce as a way of defeating the otherwise inexorable march of time, Shakespeare at once underscores the transience of physical beauty and indicates that beauty deserves and demands reproduction. In Shakespeare, and in early modern culture more generally, then, children become the focus of immense hopes and anxieties about the future. Indeed, in a culture obsessed with ancestry and descent, children literally embody the future, of an individual, of a family lineage, or of the kingdom. The isolated and unreproductive self is in these poems imagined as a form of pathology, guilty either of narcissism (Sonnet 3), miserliness (Sonnet 4), or even "murd'rous shame" (Sonnet 9, line 14). As the speaker tells the Young Man in Sonnet 13: "you know / You had a father: let your son say so" (lines 13–14). The self exists, and achieves value, in relationships, and in a temporal continuum. In a hereditary aristocracy such as early modern England, moreover, one achieves status by looking backward at ancestors, and aspires to immortality looking forward to progeny.

Critics repeatedly suggest that Shakespeare in these first nineteen poems urges a young man to marry, but there is little in these poems about the institution of marriage. Sonnet 9 does ask the Young Man if he "consum'st thyself in single life" because he does not want "to wet a widow's eye," but this seems largely intended to set up the metaphor of the world as "a makeless wife" if he died "issueless" (lines 4–6). Rather, these poems only urge him to reproduce, in order to preserve his beauty. For all of their extensive talk about love, marriage does not really come up as an important issue in the Sonnets until the beautiful sonnet beginning "Let me not to the marriage of true minds / Admit impediments" (Sonnet 116, lines 1–2; analyzed in the next chapter). And, even then, marriage is only a metaphor for a particular and special form of conjunction between humans. The speaker of Sonnet 1 promises that the production of progeny would preempt two forms of consumption identified by the poem: the young man who "Feed'st [his own] light's flame with self-substantial fuel," and who, by doing so, is a "glutton" (line 6) who would "eat the world's due" (line 14).

In Sonnet 1, progeny is likened to memory, both of which are "born," in the hope that "His tender heir might bear his memory" (line 4). Both memory and progeny, moreover, inscribe what time would eradicate, and augment what time would consume. In this way, the poet's effort to find a medium of memory is related to the reproductive strategies he urges on the Young Man. Haunted by the fact of mortality, and the passing of time, the Sonnets develop a series of provisional responses to the universal predation of time. Time is for Shakespeare an inveterate enemy, and procreation offers one kind of counter-attack. Sonnet 5 invokes "never-resting time" as a menacing figure whose industry perniciously leads summer to "hideous winter." A sunnier poet might have chosen here to emphasize the circular nature of Time, or even to delineate the subsequent transition from winter to summer, but that is not the mood of the Sonnets. Sonnet 63 refers to "Time's injurious hand" (line 2) and imagines a figure who keeps company with death and "all-oblivious enmity" (Sonnet 55, line 9).

Sonnet 115 imagines that time is a major influence on the loss of faith in humans:

> But reckoning time, whose million'd accidents
> Creep in 'twixt vows and change decrees of kings,
> Tan sacred beauty, blunt the sharp'st intents,
> Divert strong minds to the course of altering things.
>
> (lines 5–8)

It is as if the author of the Sonnets were in complete agreement with the injured Lucrece, who rails at Time as an accessory in her rape, and finally an agent in all sin and crime:

> carrier of grisly care,
> Eater of youth, false slave to false delight,
> Base watch of woes, sin's pack-horse, virtue's snare;
> Thou nursest all and murder'st all that are.
>
> (*Lucrece*, lines 926–29)

But instead of just railing against time, the poet of the Sonnets seeks out various bulwarks against what Sonnet 77 terms "Time's thievish progress to eternity" (line 8). In the early poems in particular, progeny provides an opportunity to extend a transient self into the future via other transient selves, and so achieve at least a provisional victory over time.

Shakespeare, then, begins by asking the Young Man to reproduce, but soon aspires to representational commemoration through the formal demands of poetry. Indeed, Shakespeare talks about music, and implies the music of verse, in Sonnet 8. The speaker of Sonnet 8 imagines the Young Man as someone like Duke Orsino at the beginning of *Twelfth Night*, taking indulgent pleasure in listening to sad music.

Music to hear, why hear'st thou music sadly?
Sweets with sweets war not, joy delights in joy:
Why lov'st thou that which thou receiv'st not gladly,
Or else receiv'st with pleasure thine annoy?
If the true concord of well-tuned sounds,
By unions married, do offend thine ear,
They do but sweetly chide thee, who confounds
In singleness the parts that thou shouldst bear.
Mark how one string, sweet husband to another,
Strikes each in each by mutual ordering;
Resembling sire and child and happy mother,
Who, all in one, one pleasing note do sing:
Whose speechless song being many, seeming one,
Sings this to thee: "Thou single wilt prove none."

The aesthetic question of why we enjoy sad music quickly gives way to yet another rhetorical occasion for persuading the Young Man to reproduce. The speaker reminds the Young Man that the music he loves is not made of a single string but rather is the harmonious product of many strings, which together resemble "sire, and child, and happy mother." The unity of one among many – "who all in one, one pleasing note do sing" – presages the mystical unity that Shakespeare will explore in "The Phoenix and Turtle" (to be explored in chapter 7). By praising the *discordia concors*, the harmony from difference that produces the beautiful tension of music, the poem urges the Young Man to engage in the physical unity of two beings becoming one in intercourse that produces progeny.

The opening poems advance surprisingly cynical accounts of the role of women in the processes by which males reproduce themselves. Where most previous love poetry had been dedicated to the fulsome praise of females, Shakespeare in these opening poems treats them as little more than reproductive machines, useful for incubating more males, but not worthy of the kinds of profound emotional commitment to which the poems are dedicated. Sonnet 3 imagines a woman largely as a womb that would be blessed by the "tillage" of the Young Man (line 6), while Sonnet 16 describes the "many maiden gardens" which "With virtuous wish would bear your living flowers" (lines 6–7).

As we saw, in Sonnet 1 the speaker criticizes the Young Man for a kind of narcissism approaching onanism in his being "contracted to [his] own bright eyes" (line 5). In Sonnet 4, the speaker likewise accuses the Young Man of "having traffic with thyself alone" (line 9), and in Sonnet 6 he tells him to "be not self-willed" (line 13). Sonnet 3, though, cleverly turns the narcissism of the

Young Man back upon him, suggesting that children would make a far more effective mirror, particularly when he is old:

> Look in thy glass and tell the face thou viewest
> Now is the time that face should form another;
> Whose fresh repair if now thou not renewest,
> Thou dost beguile the world, unbless some mother.
> For where is she so fair whose unear'd womb
> Disdains the tillage of thy husbandry?
> Or who is he so fond will be the tomb
> Of his self-love, to stop posterity?
> Thou art thy mother's glass and she in thee
> Calls back the lovely April of her prime;
> So thou through windows of thine age shalt see,
> Despite of wrinkles this thy golden time.
> But if thou live, remember'd not to be,
> Die single and thine image dies with thee.

The implicit threat of the couplet collapses the idea of progeny into the space of memory. In these early sonnets, it seems, selves are valued largely for their ability to extend themselves into the future via heterosexual reproduction; immuring oneself in a closed circuit of self-regard is frowned upon.

Sonnet 4 injects an economic note into the discussion, calling the Young Man a "profitless usurer" (line 7) who fails to accrue the interest of progeny on his account of beauty because he has "traffic with thyself alone" (line 9). Sonnet 6 develops the economic imagery even further, leading Shakespeare, the author of *The Merchant of Venice*, and himself an inveterate money-lender, to develop a defense of usury:

> That use is not forbidden usury,
> Which happies those that pay the willing loan;
> That's for thyself to breed another thee,
> Or ten times happier, be it ten for one.

(lines 5–8)

For the poet, the Young Man's resistance to reproduction is the moral equivalent of a miser sitting on a sum of money that could be loaned to others in ways that would enrich both the owner and those to whom it is loaned. The notion of heterosexual copulation as usury is also deployed in Sonnet 20, a poem that will be explored in detail in the next chapter. In the conclusion to Sonnet 20, Shakespeare returns to the usury of progeny to separate out the different economies of same-sex and heterosexual coupling: "But since she [Nature] pricked thee out for women's pleasure, / Mine be thy love, and thy love's use their treasure" (lines 13–14). The speaker gets the love of the Young Man, presumably in all its myriad forms, but his female lovers get the "use," or interest, of children as well.

Much of the aesthetic challenge for Shakespeare in these first nineteen poems is saying the same thing over and over again in fresh and interesting ways. Even as they endorse reproduction and copying, these poems confront the aesthetic problems that copying reveals. The last line of Sonnet 9 tells the Young Man that, by not reproducing, he "on himself . . . murd'rous shame commits." Sonnet 10 begins by picking up the concept of shame: "For shame deny thou bear'st love to any." Throughout the collection, certain contiguous poems are tightly linked in a kind of conversation in just this way. Where Sonnet 9 asks if the Young Man remains single in order to avoid making a widow grieve, Sonnet 10 capitalizes on the emotional relationship between the speaker and the Young Man: "Make thee another self for love of me" (line 13). Sonnet 12 announces in its conclusion: "Nothing 'gainst time's scythe can make defence / Save breed to brave him, when he takes thee thence." The emotions are so transparent and earnest here that it is easy to miss the strangeness of the request: the speaker asks that the Young Man, out of love for him, have sex with a woman. As we will see in the next chapter, this scenario – the possibility of a beloved male having sex with a "dark" lady – will be an occasion not of comfort but rather of despair. But in these early poems the affection between the speaker and the Young Man is largely unthreatened by the prospect of the Young Man's physical and emotional involvement with another. Indeed, the tenderness of these poems is frequently marked by terms of endearment drawn from erotic engagement. "Dear my love," says the speaker of Sonnet 13, invoking the emotional attachment articulated in Sonnet 10 ("for love of me") to persuade the Young Man to produce a son: "you know / You had a father: let your son say so" (lines 13–14).

For Shakespeare, then, time is no cloudy abstraction. Shakespeare fills these poems with trenchant images of the predations and ravages of time. The production of waste is an activity that Shakespeare seems particularly to associate with time. Sonnet 12 warns the Young Man that he ultimately "among the wastes of time must go" (line 10). The speaker of Sonnet 15 declares that time is "wasteful," and in cahoots with "Decay" (line 11). In Sonnet 16, time is a "bloody tyrant" (line 2), akin to Tarquin in his willful destruction. In both Sonnet 15 and Sonnet 16, time is a bellicose figure against whom the poet and the Young Man must declare "war."

Yet ultimately, the speaker tells the Young Man to make love not war, arguing that his best weapon in the battle with time is sexual reproduction. At the end of Sonnet 11, Shakespeare introduces a new metaphor for the reproductive practices he urges: the process by which a letter or document would be sealed by the impression in wax of an engraved stamp. Nature, the speaker advises the Young Man, "carved thee for her seal, and meant thereby / Thou shouldst print more, not let that copy die" (lines 13–14). The Young Man is like a beautiful stamp, meticulously carved by Nature herself; unlike those who are "Harsh, featureless, and rude," and so for whom a kind of natural selection allows them to "barrenly perish" (line 10), the Young Man should be used to print as many copies as possible.

Time and poetry

Although Sonnet 11 refers to the process by which a document could be authoritatively sealed by an imprint in wax – a practice that had been around for hundreds of years – the use of "print" as a verb brings up the comparatively new technology of mechanical reproduction that is the printing press. Sonnet 15, one of the most accomplished of the early sonnets, explores various organic metaphors for the processes of growth and decay before discovering a striking metaphor that is at once organic and the product of human creative endeavor:

> When I consider every thing that grows
> Holds in perfection but a little moment,
> That this huge stage presenteth nought but shows
> Whereon the stars in secret influence comment;
> When I perceive that men as plants increase,
> Cheered and cheque'd even by the self-same sky,
> Vaunt in their youthful sap, at height decrease,
> And wear their brave state out of memory;
> Then the conceit of this inconstant stay
> Sets you most rich in youth before my sight,
> Where wasteful Time debateth with Decay,
> To change your day of youth to sullied night;
> And all in war with Time for love of you,
> As he takes from you, I engraft you new.

In the couplet, the speaker engages in a horticultural metaphor that in some ways completes the various images of plants in the poems. He suggests that he will "engraft" the Young Man, which is a kind of hybrid asexual reproduction by which one inserts a shoot from one plant into the stock of another. But how he will do this depends on a multilingual pun buried in the word "engraft." The Greek word for writing is *graphein*, and the Latin term for a writing instrument is a *graphis*. The speaker is suggesting here that just as grafting gives new life to a sprig, so he will give new life to the Young Man by writing poetry about him. Like horticultural grafting, poetry is a mode of asexual propagation.

This is a subtle but apt way to announce the remarkable role that poetic verse will ultimately be assigned in the battle with time. Sonnet 16 picks up where 15 left off, asking the Young Man why he does not do his part in the war against time, especially since the battle is being fought "for love of you" (Sonnet 15, line 13). The speaker demeans his own medium of poetry as "my barren rhyme" (Sonnet 16, line 4), comparing it with a florid version of the botanical metaphors of the previous sonnet. But he then develops a complex comparison between lines of poetry and family lineage:

> Now stand you on the top of happy hours,
> And many maiden gardens yet unset
> With virtuous wish would bear your living flowers,
> Much liker than your painted counterfeit:
> So should the lines of life that life repair,
> Which this Time's pencil, or my pupil pen,
> Neither in inward worth nor outward fair,
> Can make you live yourself in eyes of men.
> To give away yourself keeps yourself still,
> And you must live, drawn by your own sweet skill.
>
> (lines 5–14)

The poem compares "the lines of life that life repair" to those drawn by the speaker's "pupil pen," and finds the latter wanting. In a bawdy pun, the poem asserts that rather than being portrayed by the poet's pen, the Young Man should "live, drawn by your own sweet skill." He compares reproduction via the poet's pen to reproduction via the Young Man's penis. The couplet asserts a complex economy related to the usury argued in Sonnet 4; there, hoarding money or semen only results in death, while investing semen or money is a model of growth.

Shakespeare continues to explore the corollary modes of reproduction in poetry and intercourse. Sonnet 17 tries to have it both ways, arguing that if the Young Man produced a child, he would have two modes of sustaining life against death: "But were some child of yours alive that time, / You should live twice; in it and in my rhyme" (lines 13–14). In the justly famous Sonnet 18, Shakespeare argues vigorously for the power of poetry to preserve the Young Man, and does so in poetry whose gentle beauty ensures its preservative powers:

> Shall I compare thee to a summer's day?
> Thou art more lovely and more temperate:
> Rough winds do shake the darling buds of May,

And summer's lease hath all too short a date:
Sometime too hot the eye of heaven shines,
And often is his gold complexion dimm'd;
And every fair from fair sometime declines,
By chance or nature's changing course untrimm'd;
But thy eternal summer shall not fade
Nor lose possession of that fair thou owest;
Nor shall Death brag thou wander'st in his shade,
When in eternal lines to time thou growest:
So long as men can breathe or eyes can see,
So long lives this and this gives life to thee.

The poem beautifully weds praise of the Young Man to the battle between poetry and time.[2] The tenderest metaphors prove inadequate to the subject of the beloved, yet in their contrived failure we are allowed to glimpse his full glory. Even as it revels in the inexpressibility of the Young Man's virtues, the poem expresses great confidence in the power of poetry; its "eternal lines" are capable of countering those of death. The brazen assertions of the couplet are deliberately arrogant, and would be misplaced in a lesser poem. But, in this extraordinary sonnet, such exorbitant claims are revealed to be not bombastic vaunting but rather unassuming fact every time it is read.

The first nineteen poems offer a sustained, compact discussion of the relationship of time and poetry, but concerns about the power of poetry and the threats of time continue to surface throughout the first 126 poems. The conclusion of Sonnet 19 strikes a triumphant tone, boldly announcing: "Yet do thy worst, old Time; despite thy wrong, / My love shall in my verse ever live young." The corollary possessives of the speaker – "my love" and "my verse" – counter the corollary possessives of time: "thy worst" and "thy wrong." In the last line, the phrase "My love," moreover, deliberately elides the emotion of the speaker with the object of that emotion. These poems inhabit a strange erotic world, one in which the Young Man will demonstrate his love for the speaker by sleeping with a woman in order to produce progeny that will preserve and continue his beauty against the decomposition of time. The poems, in other words, offer an incidental triangulation of a relationship that will in other poems in the sequence prove psychologically traumatic. Where the speaker of the first nineteen poems claims to find comfort in the Young Man's heterosexual liaisons, and even urges him to them, at other moments in the collection such triangulation results in erotic rivalry that produces immense discomfort.

The speaker of Sonnet 63 concedes that "Time's injurious hand" (line 2) will end "my lover's life" (line 12) but concludes with the surprisingly confident claim that "His beauty shall in these black lines be seen, / And they shall live, and he in them, still green" (lines 13–14). By separating out the beauty of the Young Man, eternized in poetry, from his inevitably ephemeral existence, the poet discovers a confidence in the survival of aesthetic objects. But the confidence is, like all things, short-lived. The speaker of Sonnet 65 opens by acknowledging that all things are subject to the destructive powers of time and death: "Since brass, nor stone, nor earth, nor boundless sea, / But sad mortality o'ersways their power" (lines 1–2). He ponders the status of beauty in a world in which all are subject to "the wreckful siege of batt'ring days" (line 6), asking: "How with this rage shall beauty hold a plea, / Whose action is no stronger than a flower?" (lines 3–4). Less confident in any earthly power's ability to forestall death's "spoil of beauty," the speaker concludes with a kind of prayer for the "miracle" that "in black ink my love may still shine bright" (lines 12–14). If time is in Shakespeare a principle of chaos and disorder, the deliberate form and order of poetry provide Shakespeare with a kind of victory.

In Sonnet 122, the speaker compares the ineffable processes of memory to writing in a material book, here called a "table," that the Young Man had given to him:

> Thy gift, thy tables, are within my brain
> Full character'd with lasting memory,
> Which shall above that idle rank remain
> Beyond all date, even to eternity;
> Or at the least, so long as brain and heart
> Have faculty by nature to subsist;
> Till each to razed oblivion yield his part
> Of thee, thy record never can be miss'd.
> That poor retention could not so much hold,
> Nor need I tallies thy dear love to score;
> Therefore to give them from me was I bold,
> To trust those tables that receive thee more:
> To keep an adjunct to remember thee
> Were to import forgetfulness in me.

The speaker of this poem appears ungrateful in giving away a gift he has received from the Young Man. Yet the speaker cleverly makes this into an occasion for exploring the respective merits of writing and memory. He argues somewhat casuistically that giving away the "tables" is a manifestation not of ungratefulness but rather love, because keeping the book would impugn his forgetfulness, suggesting he needed the book to remember the Young Man. Although different poems offer different answers to the comparison, Sonnet 122 clearly holds out for the superiority of memory lodged within the mortal body over the written "tallies" of "dear love." Behind the poem, though, is the grudging acknowledgment that "razed oblivion" will ultimately obliterate both the remembering lover and the writings of love.

Sonnet 55 is even bolder in its revulsion toward the effects of time:

> Not marble, nor the gilded monuments
> Of princes, shall outlive this powerful rhyme,
> But you shall shine more bright in these contents
> Than unswept stone besmeared with sluttish time.
>
> (lines 1–4)

The adjectives in line 4 convey visceral disgust, and also suggest that the life promised in these lines may really only be glorious when compared with time-smeared stone. The poem concludes with a bold promise that "you live in this, and dwell in lovers eyes." Cleverly, the prophecy is fulfilled every time the poem is read.

Time and love

Some poems explore the speaker's love for a young man whose beauty will decay, while others analyze the Young Man's reciprocal affection for the aging speaker. The speaker of Sonnet 32, for example, imagines his own death in a tone of melancholy far from the triumphs of Sonnets 19 and 55, and wonders what will happen to his remains – that is, both his body and his poetry – after his death. He envisages death as a moment when his material self will disintegrate – "When that churl Death my bones with dust shall cover" – and worries about the status of "These poor rude lines of thy deceased lover" (lines 2 and 4). He offers a partial resolution of the dilemma by changing the subject to the speaker's literary reputation among his fellow poets. With a stylish expression of humility that is designed to elicit admiration, the speaker asks the young man to "Reserve them for my love, not for their rhyme, / Exceeded by the height of happier men" (lines 7–8). By separating out the aesthetic success of an utterance from the sincerity of its expression, the speaker hopes that the Young Man will perhaps read the work of others "for their style" but will "read, his for his love." Yet the artful balance with which this sentiment is expressed belies the purported humility of the utterance. In this way, the speaker gets credit at once for an endearing humility, for emotional sincerity, and for the artifice he disavows.

Near the mid-point of the collection is a sequence of four poems that consider the degeneration and ultimate death of the speaker. These poems explore the same issues as the opening cluster, but find no victory in progeny nor in poetry. The first of these poems, Sonnet 71, somewhat disingenuously asks at length the Young Man not to mourn long for him:

> No longer mourn for me when I am dead
> Than you shall hear the surly sullen bell
> Give warning to the world that I am fled
> From this vile world with vilest worms to dwell:
> Nay, if you read this line, remember not
> The hand that writ it, for I love you so,
> That I in your sweet thoughts would be forgot,
> If thinking on me then should make you woe.
> O! if, I say, you look upon this verse,
> When I perhaps compounded am with clay,
> Do not so much as my poor name rehearse;
> But let your love even with my life decay;
> Lest the wise world should look into your moan,
> And mock you with me after I am gone.

The poem courageously refuses to imagine death through any of the various fictions of transcendence that his culture makes available – rather, it is just a passage from "this vile world" to "vilest worms." Part of the power of the poem is of course the deliberately disingenuous nature of the request. It tacitly asks the Young Man to mourn someone so selfless and so concerned for another. Like a parent who calls attention to his or her own suffering by saying "don't worry about me," the poem artfully manipulates its reader to do what it purports to disavow.

In Sonnet 73, one of the most celebrated of the Sonnets, Shakespeare explores the relationship between the ephemerality of life and the evaluation of what is loved. Affiliating his aging with the corollary passing of a year, of a day, and of a fire, the speaker develops a series of powerful images to convey the progressive devastations of age:

> That time of year thou mayst in me behold
> When yellow leaves, or none, or few, do hang
> Upon those boughs which shake against the cold,
> Bare ruined choirs, where late the sweet birds sang.
> In me thou see'st the twilight of such day
> As after sunset fadeth in the west;
> Which by and by black night doth take away,
> Death's second self, that seals up all in rest.
> In me thou see'st the glowing of such fire,
> That on the ashes of his youth doth lie,
> As the death-bed, whereon it must expire,

Consum'd with that which it was nourish'd by.
This thou perceiv'st, which makes thy love more strong,
To love that well, which thou must leave ere long.

The speaker imagines his own progressive decrepitude from the perspective of the Young Man who loves him. The first twelve lines seek for different images to describe the speaker's decay: first he is a tree losing his leaves (lines 1–4, with a glance at an abandoned church), then a day coming to its end (lines 5–8), and finally a fire burning itself out (lines 9–12). The cumulative portrait is one of continual enervation and diminution. The brilliant second line acknowledges in its portrait of progressive impoverishment that a branch with no leaves appears less destitute than a branch with a few leaves. The even more brilliant fourth line – one of the most famous in Shakespeare – invokes a powerful image of the loss of song (like the sonnets of the speaker), when the birds have fled for the winter. The poem spins on a triple pun involving the leaves of a tree, leaves of paper like those on which the poet writes, and leave-taking (the occasion of the poem). After this compelling if depressing portrait of the progressive enervation of existence, the couplet produces something of a surprise. While the syntax suggests a summary account of the inevitability of entropy ("This thou perceiv'st"), the semantics express the startlingly positive sentiment that love is made stronger by its acknowledgment of the inevitably temporary state of its objects. By imagining the speaker's aging through the eyes of a beloved young man, the poem (unlike Sonnet 71) manages for the most part to escape the centripetal force of its own self-pity.

Tinged with melancholy, the poems repeatedly confront the power of time to enfeeble and destroy all things. Sonnet 19 imagines time as a savage amoral force capable at once of making "sad and sorry seasons" (line 5), of disarming predators and enabling "heinous crime" (line 8); while its deprivations sometimes have accidental positive effects, such as "blunt[ing] . . . the lion's paws" and "Pluck[ing] the keen teeth from the fierce tiger's jaws," it can also "make the earth devour her own sweet brood," and even "burn the long-lived phoenix in her blood" (lines 1–4). The phoenix, a figure to whose mysteries Shakespeare would devote one of his most beautiful and enigmatic poems (discussed in detail in chapter 7), was famous as an image of rebirth, since it would periodically burn itself on a pyre in order to arise from its own ashes. But here Shakespeare imagines even the phoenix as ultimately subject to time, burning in its own blood rather than arising from its ashes. It is in fact deeply significant in these poems that Shakespeare resists a cyclical account of time such as that conventionally attached to the phoenix. It would be very easy for him to allow his seasonal imagery to extend through the dismal winter he laments into a spring of rebirth. But he refuses to do so, because he is so interested in exploring the finite linearity of a lifetime, and wringing from that precious short span whatever meaning he can.

Although the Sonnets sometimes express exorbitant claims for the eternizing power of verse, they for the most part ignore the possibility of eternal life via religious salvation. Like a sense of seasonal regeneration, this would have been incredibly easy for Shakespeare to write; he could have done such poetry in his sleep (and many of his contemporaries did). Indeed, so powerful are the religious pulls on language that it must have required a deliberate, even heroic, effort not to do so. It is remarkable that in these poems against time and decay – themes that almost demand a religious solution – Shakespeare aggressively resists the invocation of an afterlife, in which all losses are restored, and all wrongs made right.[3] Indeed, in the celebrated Sonnets 29 and 30, Shakespeare shows how redemption is for him a subjective state of emotion and thought. In Sonnet 29, the speaker is "in disgrace with fortune and men's eyes" (line 1), weeping for his plight while envying others theirs. Yet a turn in subject to the beloved offers a form of redemption:

> Yet in these thoughts myself almost despising,
> Haply I think on thee, and then my state,
> Like to the lark at break of day arising
> From sullen earth, sings hymns at heaven's gate.
>
> (lines 9–12)

Earth may still be "sullen," but by thinking intently on the beloved, the speaker is able to move from despair to joy. Shakespeare records here the immense power of thought to alter mood. Even the imagery of "heaven's gate" is simply a metaphor for the emotional exaltation that the speaker experiences when thinking of his terrestrial beloved.

Sonnet 30 has a similar plot line, where sadness suddenly gives way to comfort if not joy. In Sonnet 29, though, the turn takes place at line 10, while in Sonnet 30 it does not occur until the couplet:

> When to the sessions of sweet silent thought
> I summon up remembrance of things past,
> I sigh the lack of many a thing I sought,
> And with old woes new wail my dear time's waste:
> Then can I drown an eye, unused to flow,
> For precious friends hid in death's dateless night,
> And weep afresh love's long since cancell'd woe,
> And moan the expense of many a vanish'd sight:
> Then can I grieve at grievances foregone,

> And heavily from woe to woe tell o'er
> The sad account of fore-bemoaned moan,
> Which I new pay as if not paid before.
> But if the while I think on thee, dear friend,
> All losses are restored and sorrows end.

In this gorgeously melancholic sonnet, it is thinking about the beloved, not belief in a higher power, which promises comfort, restoration, and restitution amid the inevitable losses of life. Shakespeare uses the structures of terrestrial justice to depict the emotional balance sheet of his life and relationships. The poem works by imagining the most private of emotions – sadness and grief – in terms of a public institution: the sessions of a court. Until the resolution of the couplet, the speaker seems to be caught in a downward spiral of depression and loss. A preponderance of "o" and "w" sounds gives the poem the lugubrious music of a dirge. The poem turns on the mathematically irrational but emotionally comprehensible accounting by which the death of many "precious friends" is amply compensated for by the thought of one "dear friend."

Time and the afterlife

Only one poem in the sequence makes a clear appeal to an afterlife – Sonnet 146. This sonnet, something of an outlier in the sequence of poems identified with the Dark Lady, has one of the few significant textual problems in the Sonnets: the beginning of the second line repeats the last three words of the first.[4] Instead of a beautiful young man or a dark lady, the poem addresses the speaker's soul. The soul is imagined as a vulnerable entity surrounded by insurgent forces; the poem shows a kind of tender sympathy for the soul's uncomfortable situation. But the poem quickly becomes a comparatively conventional study in the politics of body–soul relations:

> Poor soul, the centre of my sinful earth,
> [. . .] these rebel powers that thee array,
> Why dost thou pine within and suffer dearth,
> Painting thy outward walls so costly gay?
> Why so large cost, having so short a lease,
> Dost thou upon thy fading mansion spend?
> Shall worms, inheritors of this excess,
> Eat up thy charge? Is this thy body's end?
> Then soul, live thou upon thy servant's loss,
> And let that pine to aggravate thy store;

Buy terms divine in selling hours of dross;
Within be fed, without be rich no more:
So shalt thou feed on Death, that feeds on men,
And Death once dead, there's no more dying then.

The poem feels somewhat out of place amid a series of poems dedicated to the voracious claims of lust. It also feels out of place in a collection remarkable for its refusal of religious answers to the problems of mortality, since the poem is the most overtly religious and even Christian in the volume. In a collection that makes a virtue of unconventionality, this is a highly conventional poem, espousing a surprisingly orthodox Christian position on the relative merits of bodies and souls. The sentiment embedded in its concluding paradox was available to almost every Elizabethan poet, and is not articulated with any particular verbal energy. Pivoting on the paradox that what feeds the body starves the soul, the poem interrogates the logic of investing in the things of this life, when this life is so short and meaningless compared to eternity. The worms from Sonnet 71 return for a cameo appearance, reminding us that whatever we feed the body is ultimately just food for worms.[5] Deploying a paradox that Donne would also use to conclude his famous sonnet "Death be not proud," Shakespeare imagines a time when death will be subject to death; when, as Donne declares "Death, thou shalt die."[6] The terms in which Sonnet 146 reveals its spiritual aspirations, moreover, are deeply material and economic: "Why so large cost, having so short a lease" (line 5) is merely a matter of good financial management (you don't spend a lot decorating a rental), as is the cunning recommendation to "Buy terms divine in selling hours of dross" (line 11). Eternal life proves a wiser investment than a "fading mansion" (line 6).

In their provisional struggle to stave off in formally accomplished language the harrowing transience of existence, then, the Sonnets rarely avail themselves of the answers that religion provides. The poems do use religious imagery, but mostly to plumb rather than resolve terrestrial mysteries. Whereas most poets use terrestrial imagery to express the transcendental truths of religion (George Herbert is probably the consummate example), Shakespeare uses religious mysteries to express the indelibly secular paradigms of love.[7] Sonnet 105, for example, begins by pleading: "Let not my love be called idolatry," separating his adulation for his beloved from a religious practice violently proscribed in Protestant England. Sonnet 108 compares the repeated speaking of his devotion to the utterances of religious ritual: "like prayers divine, / I must each day say o'er the very same" (lines 5–6). Sonnet 125 asks the beloved to "take thou my oblation, poor but free," aligning his secular devotion with the practices of religious sacrifice. While these passages all make reference to contemporaneous religious practices, none of them signals an implicit theological allegiance expressed in the sequence. Rather, they use the structures and vocabulary of religion to articulate a deeply secular devotion. The sequence is strikingly deliberate in its refusal to turn to theology for solutions to the dilemmas it elicits.

Outside of Sonnet 146, the final sonnet concerned with time is Sonnet 126, the supposed last of the Young Man sonnets. The poem marks a formal disruption; instead of a fourteen-line sonnet composed of three quatrains and a couplet, Sonnet 126 is composed of six rhymed couplets. The printer, perhaps primed by habit to expect yet another standard sonnet, assumed that the poem was missing two lines, and put in two lines of empty parentheses to represent the expected lines. The unusual form of the poem can perhaps be read as commentary on a life that gets cut short by time, the subject of the poem. The empty parentheses offer a wonderful visualization of the absences that time repeatedly creates. The poem is addressed to "my lovely boy" (line 1), a term that could either designate the Young Man addressed in the first 125 poems, or the Cupid who is subject of the last two sonnets (153 and 154). The poem, moreover, is concerned with the work of Nature, here imagined as the "sovereign mistress over wrack" (line 5). As such, the poem provides a wonderful transition between a series of poems dedicated to a beautiful young man, and a group of poems depicting a relationship with a woman possessing dark hair and morals:

> O thou my lovely boy, who in thy power
> Dost hold Time's fickle glass, his sickle hour;
> Who hast by waning grown, and therein show'st
> Thy lovers withering as thy sweet self grow'st –
> If Nature (sovereign mistress over wrack)
> As thou goest onwards still will pluck thee back,
> She keeps thee to this purpose, that her skill
> May Time disgrace, and wretched minutes kill.
> Yet fear her, O thou minion of her pleasure:
> She may detain, but not still keep, her treasure!
> Her audit (though delayed) answered must be,
> And her quietus is to render thee.
> (   )
> (   )

Like the lovely boy who seems to have time "in thy power" (line 1), the poem itself is subject to the temporal forces it describes, waning and withering before our very eyes. The Young Man flourishes as the poet ages, just as

Cupid's conquests increase as the numbers of his lovers increase. But the poem concludes with a warning that both will be subject to the final reckoning of Nature and death. Death presents an amazing blend of certainty – we all know we will die – and the unknown, since no one really knows what death means. This is what Hamlet means when he calls death the undiscovered country from which no traveler returns (*Hamlet*, 3.1.79–80).

Time and mortality are crucial subjects of the Sonnets. The poems propose the partial compensations of poetry, progeny, and memory against time's relentless and pervasive devastation. But a sense of melancholy abides, in part because of the repeated acknowledgment of death's tyrannical and final authority. Poetry, progeny, and memory begin to pale as compensations when one is dealing with the potential loss of a unique being to whom one is emotionally attached, not something that can be replicated in poetry and progeny. If everything that lives must die, the poems finally ask, what is the point of loving? Shakespeare's asking of the question, and his various answers, will be the subject of the next chapter. In Sonnet 81, the poet proudly proclaims: "Your name from hence immortal life shall have / Though I (once gone) to all the world must die" (lines 4–5). It is one of the great ironies of literary history that the identity of the object of the speaker's affection is relegated to unsubstantiated historical gossip, while the poetic statements of the speaker's affection are some of the more treasured utterances in English poetry. What Shakespeare wants to commemorate in these poems is not so much a mere name, but something far more ephemeral and volatile – the matrix of complex and conflicted emotions aroused by another person. As we will see in the next chapter, it is the turbulent love he feels for the Young Man and the disturbing passion he experiences for the Dark Lady that drive the poems, giving them their interest and energy. Focusing on the transient desires that thrill and trouble both body and soul, Shakespeare deploys all the moral force of judgment from religion but few of its gestures of transcendence to plumb the depths of human appetite and motive.

Chapter 6

Friendship and love, darkness and lust

Desire in the Sonnets

> Love is friendship set on fire.
>
> – Jeremy Taylor

Time, the subject of the last chapter, matters so much to the poet of the Sonnets because it destroys everything we love and value. It assaults beauty, and enfeebles the subjects and objects of desire. Time, in other words, is important to Shakespeare because of its destructive relationship to the objects of our central emotional commitments. Haunted by transience, Shakespeare nonetheless resists the easy religious arguments about a transcendent afterlife that are at his fingertips, and that were the occasion of comfort for many lesser poets. Almost every sonnet in the 1609 Quarto deals in some way with some form or aspect of emotional attachment. Yet Shakespeare makes the sonnet cycle something more ethically complex than anything produced by previous writers. Beginning with a male speaker imploring a beautiful young man to reproduce, and concluding with a series of poems – the "Dark Lady" poems – that affiliate heterosexual intercourse with uncontrollable passion and incurable disease, Shakespeare's Sonnets radically disrupt the conventional heterosexual narrative of erotic commitment.

I would argue, though, that critics have sometimes made too much out of the divide between the Young Man poems and the Dark Lady poems, idealizing or over-simplifying the relationship with the former in order to denigrate or complicate the relationship with the latter.[1] As we shall see, the Dark Lady poems only explore in a different tone the same concerns about the status of desire and stability of the self that run through the Young Man poems. Passion is in both relationships a rich and disturbing experience.

As we saw in the last chapter, the Sonnets do not imagine women as conventional objects of rhapsodic attention; rather, in Shakespeare's Sonnets, women are either a necessary means of biological reproduction or the trigger of intemperate lust. The vagaries of male friendship in all of its forms, from solicitous deference to ardent eroticism, absorb and transform the conventional energies of heterosexual idealization. The expressions of impassioned intimacy that inhabit most traditional sonnet sequences, by contrast, exist almost exclusively in sonnets whose addressee is a young man, or in poems whose audience is not specified. The Sonnets will range from the tender mercies implicit in the "marriage of true minds" in Sonnet 116 to the savage physiology of orgasm explored in Sonnet 129. Shakespeare offers an account of love that is sometimes idealized, sometimes brutal. Much of the immense power of the collection derives precisely from the nuanced expression of that vast expanse of attitudes to the erotic experience.

Like Shakespeare's plays, the Sonnets are fascinated by the apparent irrationality of erotic choice, and by the ways in which such choices tend to ignore or abrade various social norms and ethical expectations. The poems wonder how something so apparently ephemeral as erotic desire can produce anything that abides. They also wonder how something so intrinsically pleasurable as love can become the site of tortuous frustration or painful betrayal. They see affection for another as a kind of appetite, but worry, as Shakespeare did throughout his career, about what happens to the affection when the appetite is sated. Even as they articulate the impenetrability of the mystery of desire, they offer penetrating descriptions of its irresistible power.

In the last chapter, we looked at how Shakespeare in several poems responds to mortality by projecting the imagined relations between an inevitably fleeting present moment and a future embodied in progeny. He finds provisional comfort and stability in the possibility of populating the future. In this chapter, we will examine those poems in which Shakespeare explores the sometimes frightening, always precipitous, typically frenzied intimacy of erotic love in a poetic genre whose formal demands are premised on the idea of control. If the chosen formal constraints of the sonnet are about anything, it is the effort to impose pattern and form on the chaos of existence. Whatever stability and comfort the speaker can find will emerge from his handling of deeply unstable emotions within the formal liturgy of the sonnet. Fascinated by the continuing conflict between the curbs imposed by reason and the abandonment pursued by passion, Shakespeare explores the terrifying vulnerability of loving another being amid the painful realization of likely infidelity and certain death.

Poetry in general, and the taut form of the sonnet in particular, offers an apt medium for investigating these conflicts. The exacting structure of the sonnet encourages the meticulous articulation of urgent desires amid a restrictive series of formal demands. In this way, the form of the sonnet enacts an aesthetic version of the ethical dilemma experienced by the human who endures the contrary pulls of reason and desire. On both planes, one must find a way to meld the impulsive claims of disorderly desire with the scrupulous demands of external norms.

The master-mistress: Sonnet 20

In Sonnet 20, Shakespeare offers a kind of genealogy of erotic desire, which demonstrates a complex and roiled relationship between same-sex and heterosexual desire. The poem is in part a mini-Ovidian narrative like *Venus and Adonis*, explaining how the Young Man came to possess a beauty typically associated with women:

> A woman's face with Nature's own hand painted
> Hast thou, the master-mistress of my passion;
> A woman's gentle heart, but not acquainted
> With shifting change, as is false women's fashion;
> An eye more bright than theirs, less false in rolling,
> Gilding the object whereupon it gazeth;
> A man in hue, all "hues" in his controlling,
> Much steals men's eyes and women's souls amazeth.
> And for a woman wert thou first created;
> Till Nature, as she wrought thee, fell a-doting,
> And by addition me of thee defeated,
> By adding one thing to my purpose nothing.
> But since she prick'd thee out for women's pleasure,
> Mine be thy love and thy love's use their treasure.

Sonnet 20 certainly shows just how easy, even "natural," same-sex desire was imagined to be by early modern writers, since the poem tells the story of a feminized Nature doting erotically on her own female creation. Yet the poem also indicates a slight preference for heterosexuality, if only for reasons of convenience. Nature initially fancies a young woman, then adds a penis to the young woman in order to make her own desire suit what seems to have been the only legible form of erotic congress between women imaginable by men in the period – phallic penetration.² The bawdy puns on "thing" and "prick" underscore Nature's efforts to make her own desire conform to these male ideas of female pleasure. But Nature's prosthetic augmentation becomes the speaker's erotic frustration. Like the mystical mathematics of erotic bonds that Shakespeare explores in "The Phoenix and Turtle" (explored in chapter 7), Nature's adding a prick to the beautiful youth is for the speaker a kind of subtraction: "adding one thing to my purpose nothing." It is important to note, though, that neither Nature nor the speaker denies or disavows same-sex desire; they just find it slightly inconvenient.

This poem has been frequently used to make a case for Shakespeare's sexual proclivities. It has been cited as proof that Shakespeare was homosexual, and as evidence that he was heterosexual.³ We would perhaps do better to use the poem not as a window on Shakespeare's sex life but rather as a way to begin to understand the somewhat different configuration of sexual desire in early modern England. This is, first of all, a sexual regime in which the genitals have a supplementary rather than originary relationship to desire, and to identity. They are a crucial supplement, certainly, but not the central place where desire or identity is thought to originate. This configuration may have made more credible some Elizabethan stage conventions that can be difficult for contemporary audiences to swallow, such as the adoption of women's roles by young boys, and the related dramatic trope of cross-dressing as a convincing disguise.⁴

Sonnet 20's slightly peculiar form, moreover, is connected to this particular configuration of identity and desire. As I mentioned in chapter 1, Sonnet 20 is the only sonnet written exclusively in what is called (in Shakespeare's time and today) "feminine" rhyme. Perhaps by doing this, Shakespeare is offering a metrical equivalent to the changed sex of the youth. Even as one extra syllable per line makes for "feminine" rhyme, so does adding one "thing" in the poem constitute masculine identity. Linking its form to its content, the poem suggests thereby that sexual identity might be as fungible as meter, and as extrinsic as attire; not completely separate from genitalia, but not tied too closely to them.

Indeed, the conclusion of Sonnet 20 suggests that the possible arrangement may be that the speaker and the Young Man will share a loving relationship which does not exclude the physical, but which cannot produce children, while the Young Man will also have relationships with women (the plural "their" is interesting, and indicative of something beyond conventional marriage) in which the use-value of children will be added. As we saw in the last chapter, the principle of usury comes to stand for heterosexual reproduction; the Young Man is encouraged to reproduce through the sexual investment of semen that returns interest via progeny. Sonnet 20 also exemplifies the casual misogyny that invades so many of the Sonnets. Misogyny is of course just the flip side of the exaggerated idealization of women that constitutes so many other sonnet sequences. The speaker praises the Young Man by declaring that he is "not acquainted / With shifting change, as is false women's fashion," and possesses an eye "less false in rolling" (lines 3–5) than that possessed by the typical woman. Women in this poem are asked to set the aesthetic standard of beauty the Young Man surpasses even as they set a standard of unethical behavior that he transcends.

The marriage of true minds: Sonnet 116

Sonnet 116, by contrast, uses the ritual language of heterosexual marriage to talk about a largely spiritual relationship between two minds. The poem offers a confident but equivocal account of what love is, and what it is not:

> Let me not to the marriage of true minds
> Admit impediments. Love is not love
> Which alters when it alteration finds,
> Or bends with the remover to remove:
> O no! it is an ever-fixèd mark
> That looks on tempests and is never shaken;
> It is the star to every wandering bark,
> Whose worth's unknown, although his height be taken.
> Love's not Time's fool, though rosy lips and cheeks
> Within his bending sickle's compass come:
> Love alters not with his brief hours and weeks,
> But bears it out even to the edge of doom.
> If this be error and upon me proved,
> I never writ, nor no man ever loved.

The cerebral love the poem praises is defined by its stability and fixity. As in the sonnets explored in the last chapter, Love offers a kind of victory over Time. Sonnet 116 does concede that Time has power over "rosy lips and cheeks" (line 9), but these are apparently mere distractions for the "true minds" (line 1) that are the poem's subject. The language of the marriage ceremony in the Book of Common Prayer infuses the poem, and bestows solemnity on it; in the ritual, the married couple and the congregation would be asked if they know any "impediments" to the couple's marriage. The words "alter" and "alteration" (line 3) resonate in the poem, moreover, suggesting the "altar" before which a marriage is solemnized. In many ways, the poem celebrates what Sonnet 23 calls "The perfect ceremony of love's rite" (line 6).

This apparently confident expression of the immutability of true love, how-ever, opens up as many questions as it answers. Whose minds are being married? Is it the speaker and Young Man? This seems likely, in part because of context; the poem occurs amid a group of poems expressing love for a beautiful young man. The emphasis on the marriage of minds rather than bodies would theo-retically be available to a same-sex couple. If that is indeed the case, Sonnet 116 uses the language of the marriage service as a metaphor for faithful affection between men. But why then would the speaker be tempted to "admit imped-iments" (line 2), an activity that would be far more emotionally appropriate if the Young Man were in fact being attached to someone else? The poem's purportedly confident expressions of the fixity of true love, moreover, depend repeatedly on the process of negative definition ("Love is *not* love / Which . . ." "Love's *not* Time's fool . . ." "Love alters *not* . . .") (lines 2–3, 9, 11). A strange thing happens, moreover, when the couplet retreats into contingency: "If this be error . . ." (line 13). At once confident and precarious, the poem reveals the close connection between its eloquent idealization of love as a vital form of constancy and its abiding suspicions about love's volatile contingencies.

In Sonnet 25, the speaker celebrates a profoundly mutual erotic relationship, and takes great comfort in the confidence he feels about their reciprocal love, particularly as it is contrasted with the slippery slope of earthly fame and favor:

> Let those who are in favour with their stars
> Of public honour and proud titles boast,
> Whilst I, whom fortune of such triumph bars,
> Unlook'd for joy in that I honour most.
> Great princes' favourites their fair leaves spread
> But as the marigold at the sun's eye,
> And in themselves their pride lies buried,
> For at a frown they in their glory die.
> The painful warrior famoused for fight,
> After a thousand victories once foil'd,
> Is from the book of honour razèd quite,
> And all the rest forgot for which he toil'd:
> Then happy I, that love and am beloved
> Where I may not remove nor be removed.

The paired verbs in the couplet brilliantly underscore the profound balance of mutual affection. While others may pin their happiness on the fickle opinion of "Great princes" (line 5) the speaker rests secure in the seemingly stable love he feels and experiences.

Sonnet 25 is perhaps not a typical Shakespearean sonnet in its comfortable statement of reciprocal love. But the poem does establish a baseline of mutual affection against which other relationships in the collection can be measured. It is followed by a very different poem. Sonnet 26 uses the exaggerated language of social obligation rather than mutual affection in the effort to express an emotional bond.

> Lord of my love, to whom in vassalage
> Thy merit hath my duty strongly knit,
> To thee I send this written ambassage
> To witness duty, not to show my wit;
> Duty so great, which wit so poor as mine
> May make seem bare, in wanting words to show it,
> But that I hope some good conceit of thine
> In thy soul's thought (all naked) will bestow it,
> Till whatsoever star that guides my moving
> Points on me graciously with fair aspect,
> And puts apparel on my tattered loving
> To show me worthy of thy sweet respect.
> Then may I dare to boast how I do love thee;
> Till then, not show my head where thou mayst prove me.

The opening words of the poem – "Lord of my love" – encapsulate the poem's central question: how to unite a term of chivalric allegiance and a term of ardent affection. The words are linked by alliteration, and by a preposition. The hierarchical distance and deferential tone registers a very different relationship from the one explored in Sonnet 25. Indeed, it may well be addressed to a different audience entirely, with the context lost to history. By identifying the addressee as "Lord of my love," the speaker invokes a variant on Sonnet 20's curious term of endearment, "the master-mistress of my passion" (line 2). The two poems also share a fondness for feminine rhymes; there are three pairs of such rhymes in this poem, all in the latter half. In both poems, the political terminology emphasizes the social control that the Young Man possesses over the speaker's emotions ("master" and "lord"). Metaphorically, the terms register the social superiority the Young Man exhibits over the speaker.

Why, we might ask, should the terminology of utter subordination be asked to speak sentiments of ardent affection? In part it is conventional; the language of social courtship has long been used for erotic courtship. The linkage of service and eros is a central element of Shakespeare's Petrarchan inheritance. The Petrarchan speaker continually posits that he is the servant of his beloved, even if the gender and class dynamics of their respective status would dictate an exactly opposite relationship.[5] But Shakespeare in the Sonnets bestows new poignancy and power on the language of conventional subordination via the young man's masculine gender and superior class. And Shakespeare's fascination with the power of passion to subordinate its subject also imbues this language. Not just the range of quotidian desires and disgusts that render for us the vagaries of human character and motivation, the early modern passions were more intense and unruly than the desires that for us constitute emotion; rather, they were powerful affective impulses that the individual was thought to suffer (thus the etymology of passion from the Latin *passus*, to suffer, and its connection through *pathos* to pathology, a kind of sickness). In the early modern regime, passion always threatens to overwhelm the person who experiences it. That is one of the central reasons why a vocabulary of courtly deference is used even when the object of emotion is female, and so putatively lower on the social hierarchy.

The speaker of Sonnets 57 and 58 similarly uses the conventional language of social subordination to signify emotional commitment. Announcing that he is "your slave" and addressing his audience as "my sovereign," the speaker of Sonnet 57 describes his duty to "tend / Upon the hours and times of your desire" (lines 1, 6, 2). But, as the poem progresses, the speaker manages, through a series of negatives, to describe just how unhappy he is to serve an unfaithful master. The poem concludes with a statement of the willing self-deceptions of love: "So true a fool is love, that in your will, / Though you do anything, he thinks no ill" (lines 13–14). Both sonnets turn on the idea of waiting, a term which can involve either serving or expecting. Exaggerating the conventional masochism of the courtly lover, the speaker of Sonnet 58 disingenuously pleads:

> O, let me suffer, being at your beck,
> The imprison'd absence of your liberty;
> And patience, tame to sufferance, bide each cheque,
> Without accusing you of injury.   (lines 5–8)

The trick here is to say something in the denying of it. In the last chapter, we heard Shakespeare in Sonnet 71 covertly plead to be remembered by the friend in the very act of imploring him "No longer mourn for me when I am dead" (line 1). A different version of this tactic occurs in Sonnet 26; as the speaker declares that he writes "To witness duty, not to show my wit," he writes a consummately witty line (line 4). The conclusion of Sonnet 58 allows the vocabularies of servility and attachment to explode in frustration: "I am to wait, though waiting so be hell; / Not blame your pleasure, be it ill or well." *Pleasure* is the perfect word to mediate between the realms of servitude and affection; a servant waits "at the pleasure" of a superior, and pleasure is of course one of the central goals of an erotic relationship. The speaker, though, only experiences the "hell" that is its opposite.

These poems apply unique pressure to the highly conventional project of expressing affection in the language of social obligation; at the same time, they reveal the ways in which a language of social obligation is freighted with a tacit affective dimension. A governing idea behind such poetry is that powerful passions by definition subjugate the person who experiences them.[6] It is only a small step from the idea that powerful passion for another is inherently subjugating to the recognition that one experiences a kind of bondage to the object of one's passion. Throughout the Sonnets, Shakespeare explores the precipitous experience of erotic love in a poetic form demanding fastidious control. The result is a highly productive tension between the bridle of reason and the license of passion.

Olympian restraint: Sonnet 94

The profound subjugation advertised in this poem is the polar opposite of the cool impersonality and hyper-rationality of Sonnet 94, "They that have power to hurt and will do none." Sonnet 94 articulates a mode of self-control intended to dampen the subjugating instability of erotic passion. In Sonnet 94, Shakespeare imagines just the kind of person who is subject neither to passion nor to the influence of others. As we saw in chapter 3, Tarquin is one who has power to hurt, and does; he acts blindly on passion, and banishes reason, and damages himself and others in the process. Sonnet 94, by contrast, portrays one who acts on cold reason, and who does no harm:

> They that have power to hurt and will do none,
> That do not do the thing they most do show,
> Who, moving others, are themselves as stone,
> Unmoved, cold, and to temptation slow,
> They rightly do inherit heaven's graces
> And husband nature's riches from expense;
> They are the lords and owners of their faces,
> Others but stewards of their excellence.
> The summer's flower is to the summer sweet,
> Though to itself it only live and die,
> But if that flower with base infection meet,
> The basest weed outbraves his dignity:
> For sweetest things turn sourest by their deeds;
> Lilies that fester smell far worse than weeds.

Sonnet 94 is an atypical sonnet in many ways. There is no obvious speaker or addressee (it shares this with Sonnet 129); its generalities seem to aspire not to local advice but rather to general truth. Nonetheless, critics typically read the poem as if it were part of a longer conversation with the Young Man. Sonnet 93, the previous poem, warns the Young Man that his beauty will be a fatal attraction, like that of Eve's apple, "If thy sweet virtue answer not thy show" (line 14), while Sonnet 95 describes the "canker" that "doth spot the beauty of thy budding name" (lines 2–3). This context has led many critics to see Sonnet 94 as a reminder to the Young Man to avoid meeting with "base infection" (line 11) by exercising a kind of prophylactic self-enclosure.

I would not disagree, but I would want to extend the sonnet's message beyond the local context of these few sonnets. I would argue rather that it is a deliberately equivocal praise of a radical form of self-control that verges on hypocrisy, and that provides a kind of baseline for registering the various emotional commitments that course through the collection. Sonnet 94 exposes the uncomfortably chilly but strategically useful indifference of emotional detachment. The poem has at least as much to say to the Dark Lady poems as it does to the poems addressed to the Young Man. A largely unpleasant portrait of a highly valued trait – self-control – the poem has an impersonal tone that suits its detached subject.

The medium and message of Sonnet 94 are miles from those of the opening poems of the collection examined in the last chapter. In those poems, the speaker encouraged a young man to "Be not self-willed" (Sonnet 6, line 13); the speaker in Sonnet 94, by contrast, praises a flower that "to itself it only live[s] and die[s]" (line 10). It is tempting to read this poem as evidence of the progression of the speaker's attitude to passion, but we will resist that temptation. We will at the same time record the very different outlook on the respective claims of passion and reason manifested in the poem from those articulated in other sonnets, and use that to remind us of the provisional nature of all attitudes in the collection. Shakespeare certainly displays here a dramatist's talent for inhabiting contradictory positions in equally compelling ways. Perhaps it is not surprising that the poems would express different attitudes to the contradictory economies of sexual reproduction. Like his culture, Shakespeare values passion even as he questions the impact of headlong passionate behavior, and he values reason even as he records its costs and benefits. It is particularly telling that in the poems that occur later in the collection – not just in the Dark Lady poems, but also in the poems that worry deeply about the Young Man's infidelity – there is no mention of the possible consolation of progeny, just the self-destructive compulsions of jealousy and lust. These desperate poems depict the agonizing entropy of love frustrated or betrayed, and the even more disturbing entropy of love consummated.

The Dark Lady

In their profound investigations of the passions, the Dark Lady poems are in many ways continuous with the poems that precede them. But they do explore a desire for a creature that is radically, deliberately different in three significant ways – unlike the Young Man, she is a member of the opposite sex; unlike the Young Man, she seems not to be a member of the aristocracy; and, also unlike the Young Man, her attractions belie conventional definitions of beauty. It is important to remember that these troubling, turgid sonnets are the only overtly heterosexual poems in the sequence. By juxtaposing poems to a dark lady with poems to a young man, Shakespeare asks what happens to the terminology of love and desire when its object changes radically.

The first of the Dark Lady poems, Sonnet 127 boldly signals its deliberate violations of literary and aesthetic conventions:

> In the old age black was not counted fair,
> Or if it were, it bore not beauty's name;
> But now is black beauty's successive heir,
> And beauty slandered with a bastard shame:
> For since each hand hath put on Nature's power,
> Fairing the foul with art's false borrowed face,
> Sweet beauty hath no name, no holy bower,
> But is profaned, if not lives in disgrace.
> Therefore my mistress' eyes are raven black,
> Her eyes so suited, and they mourners seem
> At such who not born fair no beauty lack,
> Sland'ring creation with a false esteem:
> Yet so they mourn, becoming of their woe,
> That every tongue says beauty should look so.

The force of the "now" in line 3 demarcates a new standard of beauty the poet is forthwith articulating and practicing, one that challenges the venerable equation of beauty with fair, or light, complexion and hair. This new aesthetic is in part a result of the introduction of cosmetics, which means that anyone is capable of "Fairing the foul with art's false borrowed face" (line 6). This process intensifies the concern in the Young Man poems with possible disjunctions between appearance and reality; as we have seen, Sonnet 93 warns the Young Man to be sure that "thy sweet virtue answer... thy show" (line 14). It is significant that the new aesthetic of blackness in Sonnet 127 sustains the conventional deployment of class-specific terms; the Dark Lady is "beauty's successive heir," while the presumably illegitimate "bastard shame" is invoked to demarcate erotic repulsion (lines 2, 3). This decidedly deviant aesthetic is articulated *via* an appropriately perverse logic; line 9 irrationally announces that the color of his mistress's eyes is a logical consequence ("Therefore") of this change in aesthetic taste.

But this poem also leaves open the question of just what "black" means here and throughout the collection. It is certainly relevant that the period saw a vogue of poems in praise of brown or black beauties.[7] The point of such poems was to display the ingenuity of the poet in finding ways to praise unconventional beauty, since the period tended to define beauty in terms of a light complexion. This is at least as much about class as it is about race, since only the upper classes could afford to avoid the sun's tanning effects. Sonnet 130, one of Shakespeare's most famous and beloved poems, participates gently in the tradition of praising unconventional beauty:

> My mistress' eyes are nothing like the sun;
> Coral is far more red than her lips' red;
> If snow be white, why then her breasts are dun;
> If hairs be wires, black wires grow on her head.
> I have seen roses damask'd, red and white,
> But no such roses see I in her cheeks;
> And in some perfumes is there more delight
> Than in the breath that from my mistress reeks.
> I love to hear her speak, yet well I know
> That music hath a far more pleasing sound;
> I grant I never saw a goddess go;
> My mistress, when she walks, treads on the ground:
> And yet, by heaven, I think my love as rare
> As any she belied with false compare.

This clever poem manages to praise the beloved without idealizing her, by negating the traditional tropes of praise. Indeed, the joke is largely at the expense of conventional love poetry, in which the mistress is either so unreal as to be impossible to love, or so obscured by metaphors of praise that she can no longer be seen.

But blackness in these poems seems to mean different things at different times. While in some poems it may entail just the complexion and hair of the beloved, in other poems blackness seem to be a judgment as much ethical as cosmetic. In Sonnet 131, for example, he tells his "tyrannous" mistress that "In nothing art thou black save in thy deeds" (line 13). The Sonnets certainly employ, even as they disturb, a hierarchy of color that predates, but that ultimately will produce, western racism.[8] For Shakespeare, the "blackness" of his mistress – her looks and her actions – produces a disjunction between desire and knowledge, between appearance and reality, that issues in a radically divided self. The speaker of Sonnet 137 berates Cupid for distorting his vision through the fog of desire: "Thou blind fool love, what dost thou to my eyes / That they behold and see not what they see?" (lines 1–2). Sonnets 46 and 47 imagine a kind of war between the eye and the heart, so the tension between vision and passion is not new to the collection. In Sonnet 46, the war between the eye and the heart is settled amicably if a bit too neatly: "mine eye's due is thy outward part / And my heart's right thy inward love of heart" (lines 13–14). But in the Dark Lady poems, the tension is intensified to breaking point, as the force of erotic desire battles with the ethical cognition of vision. At the conclusion of Sonnet 137, the speaker can only lament the disjunction between what he sees and what he knows: "In things right true my heart and eyes have erred, / And to this false plague are they now transferred" (lines 13–14). This radically divided sense of self leaves the speaker with the symptoms of an incurable and widespread sickness.

In Sonnet 138, Shakespeare exploits the fact that the same word – "lie" – can designate the flattering fabrications that lovers tell each other and the physical position in which sex commonly occurs.

> When my love swears that she is made of truth
> I do believe her, though I know she lies,
> That she might think me some untutor'd youth,
> Unlearned in the world's false subtleties.
> Thus vainly thinking that she thinks me young,
> Although she knows my days are past the best,
> Simply I credit her false speaking tongue:
> On both sides thus is simple truth suppress'd.
> But wherefore says she not she is unjust?
> And wherefore say not I that I am old?
> O, love's best habit is in seeming trust,
> And age in love loves not to have years told:
> Therefore I lie with her and she with me,
> And in our faults by lies we flatter'd be.

This sonnet brilliantly explores the lies that bind one human to another, the ways that a kind of perverse intimacy can be premised on mutual falsehood. If his lover will tell him he is young even though he is old, he will tell her she is true even though he knows she is false. The poem turns on a false comparison between the little "white" lies that most relationships demand to some degree ("you look younger than your age") and a toxic fabrication that would erode the foundation of any relationship ("I know you are unfaithful, but I will believe you are not"). The speaker is forced to separate what he believes from what he knows: "I do believe her, though I know she lies" (line 2). The lovers lie in a bed stuffed with extreme versions of the soothing accommodations that lovers frequently tell each other. The poem pragmatically asks whether we should prefer the comforting fictions of accord over the abrasive frictions of truth. The couplet seems comfortably resolved to the former, but the ethical terminology scattered throughout the poem migrates toward the latter. In reading the poem, then, we experience something of the divide between knowledge and belief suffered by the speaker.

Sonnet 152 also looks at a speaker forced to segregate belief from knowledge in order to function in an erotic relationship. Sonnet 152, however, finds far less comfort in the lies that would cloak the beloved's infidelity than does Sonnet 138:

> In loving thee thou know'st I am forsworn,
> But thou art twice forsworn, to me love swearing,
> In act thy bed-vow broke and new faith torn,
> In vowing new hate after new love bearing.
> But why of two oaths' breach do I accuse thee,
> When I break twenty? I am perjured most;
> For all my vows are oaths but to misuse thee
> And all my honest faith in thee is lost,
> For I have sworn deep oaths of thy deep kindness,
> Oaths of thy love, thy truth, thy constancy,
> And, to enlighten thee, gave eyes to blindness,
> Or made them swear against the thing they see;
> For I have sworn thee fair; more perjured eye,
> To swear against the truth so foul a lie.

The speaker compares their mutual infidelities, and claims that "I am perjured most" (line 6), not because he has been untrue to her, but because he has been untrue to himself and the truth, in claiming that she is fair and true when he knows she is neither. The labyrinthine reasoning underpins a deep sense of self-disgust. The poem conveys a nightmarish depiction of a self led by its appetites to testify against what it knows is the truth. Both the speaker's "eye" and his "I" are willingly perjured in the praise of his lover.

Sonnet 129 is filled with disgust as well, but in this poem the disgust is directed to the sexual act itself. Like Sonnet 94, Sonnet 129 is a poem without an ostensible speaker or audience. Its subject, though, is not the self-control that Sonnet 94 equivocally praised, but rather its opposite – orgasm. Indeed, it may be the first English poem to describe in detail the phenomenon and consequences of orgasm. Sonnet 129 reveals that physical consummation of erotic desire may be like "Eve's apple" invoked in Sonnet 93 (line 13), an apparent heaven of pleasure that leads men to the hell of self-disgust:

> Th'expense of spirit in a waste of shame
> Is lust in action, and till action, lust
> Is perjured, murd'rous, bloody, full of blame,
> Savage, extreme, rude, cruel, not to trust,
> Enjoyed no sooner but despised straight,
> Past reason hunted, and no sooner had,
> Past reason hated, as a swallowed bait
> On purpose laid to make the taker mad;
> Mad in pursuit, and in possession so,
> Had, having, and in quest to have, extreme,
> A bliss in proof, and proved, a very woe;
> Before, a joy proposed; behind, a dream.
> All this the world well knows, yet none knows well
> To shun the heaven that leads men to this hell.

Sounding more like a fire-and-brimstone preacher than a devout poetic lover, the speaker does not even mention a beloved. The word "love" is absent from the poem. Religious terms like "spirit," "heaven," and "hell" occur, but in contexts far from religion. "Spirit" is used here not as an analog for "soul" but rather in its proto-medical meaning of semen. "Heaven" designates the apparent bliss of orgasm, and "hell" is either an image of the vagina or an expression of pathological post-coital *tristesse*. The sonnet's convulsive syntax and rushed enjambment brilliantly enact the rash, impulsive action the poem describes. The emphatic but progressively exhausted stresses of line 4 effectively produce one of Shakespeare's least metrical lines. The pun on *waste* and *waist* underscores the poem's unflinching account of the inexorable dissipations of erotic desire. Whereas the opening sonnets tell the Young Man that "To give away yourself keeps your self still" (Sonnet 16, line 13), Sonnet 129 tells all male lovers that the physical act of giving yourself away will ultimately destroy you, morally and physically.

Lurking behind this poem may be the common early modern medical doctrine that orgasm shortened one's life by draining one of a limited amount of spirit in ejaculation. As John Donne famously writes in "Farewell to Love," "each act [of sex], they say, / Diminisheth the length of life a day."[9] But the desperate nausea Shakespeare articulates in Sonnet 129 is more than just sadness for a shortened life. The poem is about the almost imperceptible brevity of pleasure and the protracted turpitude of lust; the poem is disgusted at the way lust is but a dream, yet it makes people behave in ways that damage self and other. The ethical and physical revulsion articulated in Sonnet 129 is in many ways just the flip side of the cool self-containment described in Sonnet 94. Both are responses to the volatile and unsettling compulsions of lust.

Love and appetite

Lust is of course a form of appetite, and the Sonnets are fascinated by the phenomenon of appetite. They aspire to know how we come to desire something, and what happens when the initial desire is sated. Sonnet 129 indicates that satisfaction is just a leap from the fleeting prospect of bliss to the lingering reality of woe. The temporal dimension of pleasure in particular interests Shakespeare; he is perpetually measuring the brevity of the pleasure against the prolongation of the consequences. He is also troubled by the periodicity of desire and satiation. Sonnet 52 praises "the fine point of seldom pleasure" (line 4), a point which can be "blunt[ed]" if it is indulged too frequently. Shakespeare repeatedly describes sexual desire by analogy to food. "Therefore are feasts so solemn and so rare," reasons the speaker of Sonnet 52, "Since, seldom coming, in the long year set, / Like stones of worth they thinly placed are" (lines 5–7). Because one definition of material value derives from scarcity of resource, suggests the speaker, perhaps desire for another increases in proportion to the time they are apart. Indeed, the speaker of this sonnet discovers a comparatively happy if grammatically enigmatic conclusion: "Being had, to triumph, being lack'd, to hope." The speaker is joyously fortunate when he possesses his beloved ("Being had"), and pleasantly expectant when they are apart ("being lack'd"). The agonies of separation recorded in other sonnets (e.g., Sonnets 27, 28, 43, 44, 45) are here transformed into a kind of erotic appetizer.

In most of the Sonnets, though, the dilemmas of appetite are not so easily resolved. Sonnet 56 explores the idea of love as an appetite whose hungers should return after satiation at least as frequently as the desire for food does after eating:

> Sweet love, renew thy force; be it not said
> Thy edge should blunter be than appetite,
> Which but to-day by feeding is allay'd,
> To-morrow sharpen'd in his former might:
> So, love, be thou; although to-day thou fill
> Thy hungry eyes even till they wink with fullness,
> To-morrow see again, and do not kill
> The spirit of love with a perpetual dullness.
> Let this sad interim like the ocean be

> Which parts the shore, where two contracted new
> Come daily to the banks, that, when they see
> Return of love, more blest may be the view;
> Else call it winter, which being full of care
> Makes summer's welcome thrice more wish'd, more rare.

The poem opens with the request that a waning passion be revived. The rhyme between "fullness" and "dullness" underscores exactly the dilemma of these poems: getting what you desire dampens desire. Fullness produces dullness. Shakespeare finds deeply troubling the way that love can be blunted by exposure to exactly what one loves. This is what gives such point to his praise of Cleopatra's erotic talents in *Antony and Cleopatra*: "Other women cloy / The appetites they feed, but she makes hungry / Where most she satisfies" (*Antony and Cleopatra*, 2.2.241–43). This is for Shakespeare a near-miracle of amorous performance – the ability simultaneously to whet and sate appetite.

Sonnet 75 articulates the rhythms of a far less miraculous erotic life, again linking emotional commitment to patterns of diet: "So are you to my thoughts as food to life" (line 1). The speaker experiences the beloved as either feast or fast, and seems to experience discomfort in both:

> Sometime all full with feasting on your sight
> And by and by clean starvèd for a look;
> Possessing or pursuing no delight,
> Save what is had or must from you be took.
> Thus do I pine and surfeit day by day,
> Or gluttoning on all, or all away.
>
> (lines 9–14)

The speaker depicts a bulimic existence that staggers maddeningly from overindulgence to deprivation, amid the bitter irony that there is no middle ground of genuine satisfaction. In *The Merchant of Venice*, Nerissa suggests that "they are as sick that surfeit with too much as they that starve with nothing" (1.2.5–7). In Sonnet 75 Shakespeare investigates the even more profound sickness of one who reels from surfeit to starvation.

Indeed, the lack of control implicit in erotic desire is so profound that the speaker of Sonnet 118 views love as a kind of symptom and an actual sickness.

> Like as to make our appetites more keen,
> With eager compounds we our palate urge,
> As, to prevent our maladies unseen,
> We sicken to shun sickness when we purge,
> Even so, being full of your ne'er-cloying sweetness,
> To bitter sauces did I frame my feeding

> And, sick of welfare, found a kind of meetness
> To be diseased ere that there was true needing.
> Thus policy in love, to anticipate
> The ills that were not, grew to faults assured
> And brought to medicine a healthful state
> Which, rank of goodness, would by ill be cured:
> But thence I learn, and find the lesson true,
> Drugs poison him that so fell sick of you.

The speaker bizarrely compares the contemporaneous medical practice of alimentary purgation for the purpose of preventing disease ("sicken to shun sickness when we purge": line 4) to a kind of aperitif, a bitter sauce designed to "make our appetites more keen" (line 1). Both are cures of a sort, whose effectiveness is linked to the production of discomfort, or, in its original sense, "dis-ease." Indeed, the speaker announces that he is "sick of welfare," "diseased," and "full of your ne'er-cloying sweetness" (lines 7, 8, 5). The compound adjectival phrase brilliantly conveys the extremes of appetite between which he flounders; it can mean both "never cloying" and "near cloying," continual desire and nauseous surfeit. The poem concludes in despair, with the recognition that the speaker is poisoned by the very remedies he hopes to use to cure his love-sickness.

Love and disease

It is telling that this poem tying love to disease is not located amid the Dark Lady poems. In fact, both areas of the collection contain poems that inspect the darkest aspects of erotic commitment. In Sonnet 147, "My love is as a fever," a poem in the Dark Lady segment, the speaker identifies his "love" as a disease that threatens to destroy its host:

> My love is as a fever, longing still
> For that which longer nurseth the disease,
> Feeding on that which doth preserve the ill,
> Th'uncertain sickly appetite to please.
> My reason, the physician to my love,
> Angry that his prescriptions are not kept,
> Hath left me, and I desperate now approve
> Desire is death, which physic did except.
> Past cure I am, now reason is past care,
> And, frantic-mad with evermore unrest,
> My thoughts and my discourse as madmen's are,

> At random from the truth vainly expressed:
> For I have sworn thee fair and thought thee bright,
> Who art as black as hell, as dark as night.

Love is a disease that causes a craving for just what makes the patient sicker. A minor allegory of the self emerges in the second quatrain: Reason is the physician, but is frustrated, because the speaker is a patient who refuses to follow the prescriptions. The speaker confesses to a profoundly conflicted sensibility that verges on insanity. Appetite is "uncertain" and "sickly," and "Desire is death" (lines 4, 8). In this poem, finally, erotic desire offers not the refuge from the ravages of time and death that is claimed in other sonnets. It is, rather, only a venue for hastening time's grievous mortal effects: "desire is death."[10] The penultimate line of the poem begins just as the penultimate line of Sonnet 152 does: "For I have sworn thee fair." In both poems, the speaker is tormented by the dissociation between what he has sworn and what he knows.

Another sonnet in the Dark Lady segment imagines not only that desire is a disease, but also that it is highly contagious. Sonnet 144 identifies an explicit love triangle in which the speaker is enmeshed, and uses the striking image of a psychomachia, in which angels and devils battle for a soul, to depict the two different erotic pulls he feels:

> Two loves I have of comfort and despair,
> Which like two spirits do suggest me still:
> The better angel is a man right fair,
> The worser spirit a woman colour'd ill.
> To win me soon to hell, my female evil
> Tempteth my better angel from my side,
> And would corrupt my saint to be a devil,
> Wooing his purity with her foul pride.
> And whether that my angel be turn'd fiend
> Suspect I may, but not directly tell;
> But being both from me, both to each friend,
> I guess one angel in another's hell:
> Yet this shall I ne'er know, but live in doubt,
> Till my bad angel fire my good one out.

Completely inverting the overt sexual hierarchies of Christianity, the speaker describes his male lover as an angel and his female lover as a devil. Same-sex love is here seen as more blessed than heterosexuality. Shakespeare, moreover, gives the conventional psychomachia an unconventional wrinkle: he envisions the possibility that the devil might seduce the angel; his female lover would have sex with his male lover. The speaker is troubled by the possibility, and even more troubled that he cannot know for sure (this is of course the poet who wrote *Othello*, that harrowing account of the agony of erotic uncertainty). Yet in the conclusion he envisions a way of knowing whether his female and male lovers have been unfaithful to him with each other, but it offers him no comfort: if his bad angel "fire[s]" his good one "out" – that is, infects him with venereal disease – then he will no longer "live in doubt" (lines 14, 13). The poem offers a disquieting take on the comfortable scenario envisioned at the end of Sonnet 20, whereby the speaker would receive the love of the Young Man, and women would receive his "love's use" (line 14).

Behind the connection between the heat of sexual passion and the fire of disease exploited in both Sonnets 144 and 147 is the idea that venereal disease is actually caused by an abundance of sexual passion. A culture that lacked any notion of bacterial infection nevertheless knew that it could spread from one person to another, but imagined this process as the contagion of desire rather than the physical transmission of pernicious biological organisms. A passage in *Venus and Adonis* describes sexually transmitted disease as "The marrow-eating sickness whose attaint / Disorder breeds by heating of the blood" (lines 741–42). As Donne remarks in "The Paradox," "Love with excess of heat, [kills] more young than old."[11] Heat is both symptom and cause of desire. And, as we will see in the last sonnets in the collection, it is spread through the very technologies designed to cool it off.

If there really is a dark lady, then, Shakespeare portrays a speaker who is at once afraid of and drawn to the dark. It is important to note that although it may begin with her complexion and hair, the darkness that inhabits the poems about her lurks in the desires she arouses as much as in the lady herself. These poems about the irrational and uncontrollable aspects of desire articulate a pronounced fear that humans are little more than a composite of appetites they can barely control. Exploring this fear, Sonnets 135 and 136 pun shamelessly on the felicitous fact that the poet's first name – "Will" – is also a term designating sexual desire, and even male and female sexual organs:

> Whoever hath her wish, thou hast thy Will,
> And Will to boot, and Will in overplus;
> More than enough am I that vex thee still,
> To thy sweet will making addition thus.
> Wilt thou, whose will is large and spacious,
> Not once vouchsafe to hide my will in thine?
> Shall will in others seem right gracious,
> And in my will no fair acceptance shine?
> The sea all water, yet receives rain still,

And in abundance addeth to his store;
So thou, being rich in Will add to thy Will
One will of mine, to make thy large Will more.
Let no unkind, no fair beseechers kill;
Think all but one, and me in that one Will.

At once playful and terrifying, bawdy and desperate, Sonnet 135 imagines the possibility of individual identity dissolving into undifferentiated sexual appetites, just as the speaker envisions hiding his "will" in her oceanic will. Since *Will* can designate the poet, his penis, his lust, his beloved, his beloved's lust, and his beloved's genitalia, the poems inquire whether individual identity and romantic love are simply elaborate fictions laminated on a series of disturbingly undifferentiated erotic appetites. The sonnet connects sexual and verbal promiscuity, suggesting that word play is a kind of foreplay. It is as if the speaker can almost hide his pain at the repeated infidelity of the beloved behind the proliferation of puns. In Sonnet 136, the jangling repetitions of the word "will" almost empty it of meaning, especially on the heels of Sonnet 135; the word is used 21 times in the 28 lines of the two contiguous poems. Sonnet 136 concludes as if it were a riddle poem, something like Sonnet 144, with its pun on Hathaway. "Make but my name thy love, and love that still, / And then thou lovest me, for my name is Will." But the conclusion is saturated with erotic anxiety, as the speaker hopes to turn the promiscuity of the beloved back upon her: if you follow your will (your sexual appetite), the speaker suggests, then that will lead you back to me, because my name is Will. It is a conclusion that reiterates rather than alleviates his fears about the unfaithfulness of his beloved, and the complete dissociation of physical intimacy from emotional attachment that that unfaithfulness bespeaks.

The last two sonnets in the collection are not specifically about a dark lady. Instead, they are about Cupid, leading some critics to think of them as extraneous, tacked on to the sequence. But their subject – the irrepressibility of desire – makes them an appropriate conclusion to the Dark Lady poems, and to the collection as a whole. As we might expect, there are no happy endings in Shakespeare's Sonnets – just a series of provisional and partial efforts to stave off in different media the tortuous temporality of existence through articulate expressions of the profundity of emotional attachment or through nervous assertions of the immortalizing power of poetry. The last two sonnets use the myth of Cupid to demonstrate the contagious and incurable nature of "love's fire," which is, as we have seen, passion heated to the point of a transmittable disease. Like *Venus and Adonis*, which tells the story of the reason that love will never work out happily for humans, both sonnets aspire to tell the origin of a truth about love. In Sonnet 153, Shakespeare explores the relationship between the "holy fire of love" and the "heat" of sexual passion:

> Cupid laid by his brand, and fell asleep:
> A maid of Dian's this advantage found,
> And his love-kindling fire did quickly steep
> In a cold valley-fountain of that ground;
> Which borrow'd from this holy fire of Love
> A dateless lively heat, still to endure,
> And grew a seething bath, which yet men prove
> Against strange maladies a sovereign cure.
> But at my mistress' eye Love's brand new-fired,
> The boy for trial needs would touch my breast;
> I, sick withal, the help of bath desired,
> And thither hied, a sad distemper'd guest,
> But found no cure: the bath for my help lies
> Where Cupid got new fire – my mistress' eyes.

A maid of Diana, the goddess of chastity, spies a sleeping Cupid, and steals his brand, hoping to douse forever the fire of passion "in a cold valley-fountain" (line 4). But instead of cooling off Cupid's brand, the water is heated by it, and becomes a hot spring like that which the period imagined could cure venereal disease by having the sufferer sweat out the pernicious passion. The speaker finds, moreover, that Cupid found new fire in the "mistress' eye" (line 9). The ocular foreplay that had been such a central part of Petrarchan love poetry emerges at the end of the poem to rekindle the desire, and the disease, for which the speaker initially seeks a "cure." This was, of course, a culture that believed in love at first sight, in large part because of the capacity for eyes to provoke the spontaneous combustion of erotic desire.

The last sonnet demonstrates yet again how, in the universe of Shakespeare's Sonnets, the effort to contain or cure love just offers further opportunities for its proliferation:

> The little Love-god lying once asleep
> Laid by his side his heart-inflaming brand,
> Whilst many nymphs that vowed chaste life to keep
> Came tripping by; but in her maiden hand
> The fairest votary took up that fire
> Which many legions of true hearts had warmed,
> And so the general of hot desire
> Was sleeping by a virgin hand disarm'd.
> This brand she quenched in a cool well by,
> Which from Love's fire took heat perpetual,

> Growing a bath and healthful remedy
> For men diseased; but I, my mistress' thrall,
> Came there for cure, and this by that I prove:
> Love's fire heats water, water cools not love.

Desire, Shakespeare suggests, is a kind of universal solvent, corroding whatever is supposed to contain it. It is, moreover, a highly contagious disease, and one that spreads through the very therapies intended to cure it. The "heart-inflaming brand" has obvious erotic possibilities, as does the "cool well" in which it is quenched (lines 2, 9). The resemblance of the image for containing desire to the image for consummating desire adumbrates exactly the point of the poem: that desire cannot be dampened or contained. The brand heats up the well rather than the well cooling off the brand. As in the previous poem, it is relevant that a leading therapy for venereal disease in the period was to go to the baths.[12]

Shakespeare had been fascinated by the idea that desire cannot be denied since his first publication, *Venus and Adonis*, where Adonis' resistance is made to seem a bit perverse in an amoral world animated by lust. The idea is also a major element in *Love's Labour's Lost*, that early comedy in which four men renounce all female companionship in order to pursue the "higher" aspirations of knowledge, but who of course fall immediately in love and lust. Throughout his career, Shakespeare was fascinated by the dynamic tension between detachment and sensibility, between self-control and attachment. For Shakespeare, the danger of refusing to feel is almost as great as the danger of allowing feelings to subjugate one.

In these last two sonnets, the constancy that would typically be praised in conventional sonnets comes back to haunt the speaker. Cynically, the poems suggest that desire is a kind of phoenix (an image that Shakespeare will explore in "The Phoenix and Turtle"), and will repeatedly arise from its own ashes. Just when one hopes to shut it down, desire comes back with a vengeance. This pattern of rebirth proves for Shakespeare both a blessing and a curse. These playfully bleak sonnets are followed in the 1609 volume by *A Lover's Complaint*, the grief-stricken lament of an abandoned female lover who confesses in the poem's final line that she would do it all again if given the chance. This poem is in part a cynical response to Spenser's glorious celebration of the consummation of his erotic desire in the *Epithalamion* that follows his sequence of love sonnets, the *Amoretti*. As we shall see in the next chapter, the poem provides an apt conclusion to the sonnet sequence, underscoring the internal agonies, obsessive behaviors, ephemeral joys, and compulsive behaviors of love. But we will also look closely at "The Phoenix and Turtle," a deeply enigmatic poem in which

Shakespeare nonetheless seems to imagine a very different set of possibilities for human relationships than those which the Sonnets and *A Lover's Complaint* leave us. Whereas the Sonnets and *A Lover's Complaint* provide an unblinking account of the compulsive pleasures of erotic commitment, "The Phoenix and Turtle" will use the language and rituals of religion to describe the tragic mysteries of a truly mutual love.

Chapter 7

Solitary and mutual flames

A Lover's Complaint and "The Phoenix and Turtle"

> The Phoenix riddle hath more wit
> By us; we two being one are it.
>
> – John Donne

This chapter will focus on two very different poems, with hugely different perspectives on love. Both are part of larger collections, and both acquire some of their meaning through their specific contexts: *A Lover's Complaint* was printed in 1609 at the end of the Sonnets (although it is not mentioned on the title page of the volume), and "The Phoenix and Turtle" was published in 1601, in a collection of verses by various writers appended to a volume entitled *Love's Martyr*. "The Phoenix and Turtle" is an abstruse semi-philosophical work that uses the literary idea of a meeting of various species of birds to explore the paradoxical unity achieved by two separate beings through love. *A Lover's Complaint* is the grief-stricken lament of an abandoned female lover. Both poems show Shakespeare inhabiting and exploding inherited genres and modes. If "The Phoenix and Turtle" is Shakespeare sounding like John Donne at his best, *A Lover's Complaint* is Shakespeare sounding like Edmund Spenser on a good day (something he also does in Sonnet 106). One recent critic has judged *A Lover's Complaint* as unworthy of Shakespeare, and has argued vigorously that the poem is not by him.[1] There have been fewer questions about the authorship of "The Phoenix and Turtle," despite the fact that the circumstances of publication are similar. Perhaps this is because "The Phoenix and Turtle" is universally acknowledged as a small masterpiece; the poem has been aptly termed "the first great published metaphysical poem."[2] This chapter will operate under the widely held assumption that both poems, published while Shakespeare was still alive and attributed to him in print, are indeed by him. Unable to know with certainty the chronology of composition, we will distort the chronology of publication, and look first at *A Lover's Complaint*, acknowledging its proximity to the Sonnets, and its formal similarity to *Venus and Adonis* and *Lucrece*. We will then explore "The Phoenix and Turtle," noting its anomalous form and uncharacteristically occult content. Both poems investigate the origins of desire, and both poems ask what is left when desire, or the objects of desire, vanish.

A Lover's Complaint

A Lover's Complaint comes on the heels of the playfully bleak sonnets about Cupid that conclude the 1609 volume. We move from a mischievous Cupid who spreads irrational passion like a disease to the grief-stricken lament of an abandoned female. As different as they are in type, though, the poems are similar in message; just as Sonnets 153 and 154 show how love spreads in the very act of trying to dampen it, the female speaker of *A Lover's Complaint* confesses in the poem's final line that she would do it all again if given the chance. It is as if the very telling of her tale of woe made her remember all its seductive attractions, and feel again their pull.

Shakespeare was not the first poet to conclude a sequence of sonnets with a longer poem. One of Shakespeare's primary models, Samuel Daniel, had ended his sonnet sequence *Delia* (1592) with *The Complaint of Rosamund*, a fictional complaint by an injured female. Edmund Spenser, by contrast, had ended his *Amoretti* (1595) with the celebratory *Epithalamion*, a glorious celebration of the consummation of erotic desire through marriage. *A Lover's Complaint* is far more closely aligned with Daniel's example than with Spenser's. Where Spenser proclaims the successful conclusion of his lyric courtship with a wedding song, Daniel's *Complaint* is spoken by a ghost who longs to tell her tale of amorous woe. Shakespeare's complaint tells a story of erotic betrayal that seems to consummate many of the various betrayals and infidelities portrayed in the Sonnets. The poem provides an apt conclusion to the sonnet sequence, emphasizing the complex blend of apparent pleasure and actual pain that constitutes the experience of unrequited love, and offering Shakespeare an opportunity to voice, from the perspective of a female, the charms and consequences of love and sex.

The poem is written in a highly mannered style, and in the same rhyme royal stanzaic form that Shakespeare had used in *Lucrece*. Indeed, the poem shares much with that early Ovidian narrative. As in *Lucrece*, Shakespeare is fascinated by female subjectivity, particularly a voluble female who has been victimized by a male. Unlike *Lucrece*, the speaker of *A Lover's Complaint* has not been raped, just seduced. But in both poems Shakespeare finds the voice and emotions of an injured woman to be a subject of immense interest. The convention of female complaint seems to have interested male poets such as Daniel and Shakespeare in part because it allowed them to imagine the audience of the kinds of love poetry they have composed. Since *A Lover's Complaint* follows the Sonnets in 1609, it is fascinating to observe possible links between Shakespeare's persona in the sonnets and the concerns of a lamenting woman. Most significantly, both are caught in cycles of desire and despair that they feel unable to break.

The poem begins with a narrator who overhears the complaints of a woman in the distance. The landscape itself, as in *Venus and Adonis*, is richly suggestive of the bodies and pleasures of the inhabitants:

> From off a hill whose concave womb re-worded
> A plaintful story from a sistering vale,
> My spirits to attend this double voice accorded,
> And down I laid to list the sad-tuned tale;
> Ere long espied a fickle maid full pale,
> Tearing of papers, breaking rings a-twain,
> Storming her world with sorrow's wind and rain.
>
> (lines 1–7)

The phenomenon of the echoing hill and concave womb becomes a naturalistic version of the poem itself, which echoes the concerns of the previous sonnets. The "womb," of course, connects landscape geography to female anatomy. The narrator, who remains unnamed, and who drops out of the frame, is positioned something like the reader of a sonnet sequence, ostensibly overhearing either a monolog or a conversation between a poet and a lover.

The narrator spies "a fickle maid full pale"; the adjective suggests her tempest of contradictory passions. She is tearing up "papers" which are probably love letters or sonnets, and "breaking rings a-twain." She is actively destroying the courtship gifts she has received. The ring in this regard is particularly significant, since it is a typical token of erotic commitment. It might even be a posie ring, a ring with a verse on the inside; these rings were common as lover's tokens in early modern England. Even as she destroys the gifts she has received, the woman exhibits the devastation of her erotic suffering:

> The carcass of beauty spent and done:
> Time had not scythed all that youth begun,
> Nor youth all quit; but, spite of heaven's fell rage,
> Some beauty peep'd through lattice of sear'd age.
>
> (lines 11–14)

Her intense grief has aged her prematurely. Shakespeare gives us several details about her, and asks us to guess her plight from them. Her handkerchief is covered with "conceited characters" which remind her of her beloved; "reading what contents it bears" prompts her "shrieking undistinguished woe" (lines 16–20). Her eyes wander, and her hair, "nor loose nor tied," was "slackly braided in loose negligence" (lines 29, 35). The loss of control in both details adumbrates the abandonment to passion that got her into this situation in the first place; the lack of care for appearance also demonstrates the full devastation of her forlorn state.

She is throwing "A thousand favours" into a river, even as she weeps into it as well, a process that Shakespeare compares to "usury applying wet to wet," as if he wanted us to remember all those early sonnets urging the Young Man to apply the principles of usury to his own expenditure of his seminal fluid. She takes some "letters sadly penned in blood," and treats them with a combination of tenderness and rage. The letters trigger her first words in the poem:

> These often bathed she in her fluxive eyes,
> And often kiss'd, and often 'gan to tear:
> Cried "O false blood, thou register of lies,
> What unapproved witness dost thou bear!
> Ink would have seem'd more black and damned here!"
>
> (lines 50–54)

By indicating the propriety of the color of ink to her situation, Shakespeare has her invoke the same ethical hierarchy of color that drives the Dark Lady poems. As she berates the letters as a "register of lies," she invokes the blend of eroticism and prevarication that marks Sonnet 138.

She is then approached by "A reverend man" who asks "the grounds and motives of her woe," promising her that "If that from him there may be aught applied / Which may her suffering ecstasy assuage," he will do it (lines 57, 63, 68–69). It is interesting that an expression of sympathy prompts the substance of the poem, since the poem itself questions the advisability of opening oneself up to another. She tells the old man that she is not as old as she looks, and

> might as yet have been a spreading flower,
> Fresh to myself, if I had self-applied
> Love to myself and to no love beside.
>
> (lines 75–77)

The tensions between cool self-enclosure and passionate commitment played out in the Sonnets are here translated into the tragic experience of this old-looking young woman. If she had only behaved more as the Young Man does in the opening sonnets, self-applying love to herself, or as the figure exhibiting chilly self-control described in Sonnet 94, she might not now be suffering the ravages of time and care.

Her mistake, though, was that she "attended / A youthful suit" (lines 78–79) from "one by nature's outwards so commended / That maidens' eyes stuck over all his face" (lines 80–81).[3] He is very young, and lacks a beard; on his chin is only "phoenix down [which] began but to appear / Like unshorn velvet, on that termless skin" (lines 93–94). It is fascinating that the object of a desire that keeps arising from its own ashes sports "phoenix down" on his chin. The Young Man, we learn later, is so lovely that both men and women are subject to his charms: "he did in the general bosom reign / Of young, of old; and sexes both enchanted" (lines 127–28). He resembles here the Young Man described in Sonnet 20, who "steals men's eyes and women's souls amazeth" (line 8).

The Young Man is not just beautiful; he is also eloquent, "maiden-tongued," in the rich phrase through which Shakespeare imagines the young woman describing the power of the Young Man's words over her (line 100). We can assume from the phrase both that the Young Man spoke with the soft attractive grace that the culture attributed to maidens, and that his words were particularly appealing to maidens. Yet his eloquence is detached from any notions of veracity: "His rudeness so with his authorized youth / Did livery falseness in a pride of truth" (lines 104–05). The disjunction between beauty and truth explored in the Sonnets finds its corollary in the youth's winning combination of eloquence and insincerity. We are told that "his subduing tongue" had great power over others, and could "make the weeper laugh, the laugher weep" (lines 120, 124). The Young Man has power, then, not only over his own emotions, but also over the emotions of others: "He had the dialect and different skill, / Catching all passions in his craft of will" (lines 125–26). Shakespeare is here fascinated by the affective power of beautiful words and arguments detached from any necessary connection to the truth.

The youth, we are told, is also a good horseback rider, and the terms in which this talent is described relate to his impressive self-command as well as his power over others:

> Well could he ride, and often men would say
> "That horse his mettle from his rider takes:
> Proud of subjection, noble by the sway,
> What rounds, what bounds, what course, what stop he makes!"
> And controversy hence a question takes,
> Whether the horse by him became his deed,
> Or he his manage by the well-doing steed.   (lines 106–12)

At least in the eyes of his abandoned lover, the youth possesses all the skills and "grace" of a truly cavalier gentleman. She remembers that his "real" or regal "habitude gave life and grace / To appertainings and to ornament" (lines 114–15).

The abandoned woman suggests, moreover, that his graceful composure gave him great power over others. She uses the word "bewitched" to describe the way that he attains the "consent" of others "ere he desire"; those around him have been so charmed that they have "Asked their own wills [what he would say] and made their wills obey" (lines 131–33). His capacity to generate preemptive obedience in others presages the power he will exert over the lady. He also possesses the remarkable ability to make several people simultaneously feel that they are "mistress of his heart" (line 142).

It is certainly no surprise when the woman proves susceptible to his myriad charms. His winning combination of youthful beauty and verbal eloquence leads her to succumb to his seductions:

> What with his art in youth, and youth in art,
> [I] Threw my affections in his charmed power,
> Reserved the stalk and gave him all my flower.
> (lines 145–47)

The frankly sexual imagery of the flower and the stalk affiliates eroticism with the natural world, and reveals the full carnal extent of her surrender.

Yet, she tells us with some pride, she did not yield immediately, "as some my equals did" (line 148). Rather, "With safest distance I mine honour shielded" (line 151). She uses the ample evidence of "his amorous spoil" (line 154) as "bulwarks" (line 152) against his erotic assaults. She knows that "his plants in others' orchards grew," that he had produced children with other women (line 171). It is as if the youth had read the early sonnets to the Young Man urging him to reproduce, and followed the advice religiously. The woman knew that his "characters and words" were "merely but art, / And bastards of his foul adulterate heart" (lines 174–75). His words, then, resemble the illegitimate issue of his various courtships. But such ominous "precedent" finally is not enough for her, since "The destined ill she must herself assay" (lines 155–56). She discovers ominously that her own resistance only serves to whet her appetite: "For when we rage, advice is often seen / By blunting us to make our wits more keen" (lines 161–62). As happens so frequently in Shakespeare, the effort to contain desire only occasions the proliferation of desire. She experiences powerfully a dissociation of appetite from reason:

> O appetite, from judgement stand aloof!
> The one a palate hath that needs will taste,
> Though Reason weep, and cry, "It is thy last."
>
> (lines 166–68)

As in *Lucrece* and the Sonnets, we watch the thought processes of a figure who, acting against her better judgment, behaves in self-destructive ways.

As she describes his methods of courtship, she uses the traditional imagery of herself as a "city" that he "besiege[s]" (lines 176–77). It is interesting that, despite all the suffering he must have caused, he has the gall to ask for the maid's sympathy for his own pain: "Gentle maid, / Have of my suffering youth some feeling pity" (lines 177–78). Indeed, he suggests later that the women he loved and left got exactly what they wanted, and what they deserved: "They sought their shame that so their shame did find" (line 187). He does not deny his colorful past, but assimilates it brilliantly to his rhetorical goals, protesting that "All my offences that abroad you see / Are errors of the blood, none of the mind: / Love made them not" (lines 183–85). The separation of blood and mind is used to suggest a merely physical love as opposed to an engagement of true minds. This is of course one of the best ways to achieve the physical love he seeks, by flattering her into thinking just how special she is compared to all his other victims.

He even shows her the various love tokens he has received, which he calls "trophies of affections hot" (line 218). The tone and detail are worth quoting at length, so that we can see both his cold-bloodedness toward his former lovers, and the seductive power of these trinkets:

> "Look here, what tributes wounded fancies sent me,
> Of paled pearls and rubies red as blood;
> Figuring that they their passions likewise lent me
> Of grief and blushes, aptly understood
> In bloodless white and the encrimson'd mood;
> Effects of terror and dear modesty,
> Encamp'd in hearts, but fighting outwardly.
>
> "And, lo, behold these talents of their hair,
> With twisted metal amorously impleach'd,
> I have received from many a several fair,
> Their kind acceptance weepingly beseech'd,
> With the annexions of fair gems enrich'd,
> And deep-brain'd sonnets that did amplify
> Each stone's dear nature, worth, and quality.
>
> "The diamond, – why, 'twas beautiful and hard,
> Whereto his invised properties did tend;

The deep-green emerald, in whose fresh regard
Weak sights their sickly radiance do amend;
The heaven-hued sapphire and the opal blend
With objects manifold: each several stone,
With wit well blazon'd, smiled or made some moan."

(lines 197–217)

With the phrase "deep-brained sonnets" on the heels of a collection of some of the deepest-brained sonnets in any language, Shakespeare is perhaps having a bit of fun with his own poems, and the part some of them may have played in games of courtship; here he imagines that the primary function of such poetry is to "amplify / Each stone's dear nature, worth, and quality" (lines 209–10). It is telling that the poems were originally composed by the women who had sought the Young Man's erotic attentions. We are given here a glimpse of a world like that of *Venus and Adonis*, in which highly verbal women attempt to seduce beautiful young men through the tropes and conventions of erotic literature. The youth then offers to the woman the various love tokens he has received from his various lovers; he renders them, with conventionally exorbitant flattery, "to you, my origin and ender" (lines 221–22). The Young Man even finds a "device" that was given him by a nun who, after she met him, "would the caged cloister fly" (lines 232, 249). With a bit of bravado, he remembers that "My parts had power to charm a sacred nun," one "disciplined, ay, dieted, in grace" (line 260–61). If he could win over someone with such discipline and willpower, he wonders, how does the maid in front of him manage to resist his charms? As he does with everything, he cleverly turns his wonder at her resistance into flattery of the very person whose resistance he is trying to break down: "How mighty then you are" (line 253).

The youth then offers an eloquent hymn to love, which would probably be more valued in literary criticism if it were not so tainted by his motives:

"O most potential love! vow, bond, nor space,
In thee hath neither sting, knot, nor confine,
For thou art all, and all things else are thine.

"When thou impressest, what are precepts worth
Of stale example? When thou wilt inflame,
How coldly those impediments stand forth
Of wealth, of filial fear, law, kindred, fame!
Love's arms are peace, 'gainst rule, 'gainst sense, 'gainst shame,
And sweetens, in the suffering pangs it bears,
The aloes of all forces, shocks, and fears."   (lines 264–73)

Sounding a bit like the Venus of *Venus and Adonis*, the youth views love as the dynamic center of all value. Love, he says, is all-powerful (the meaning of "most potential"), and ultimately irresistible. It defies the "precepts . . . Of stale example" (lines 267–68), and is a flame that can burn through all societal hindrances. As in Sonnet 116, the word "impediments" invokes the marriage service, but here the invocation is perverse, since the youth is definitely not seeking marriage. The phrase "suffering pangs" (line 272), moreover, may invoke childbirth, which can be for a young single woman the unfortunate outcome of precisely the activity the youth is urging. The impediments to love that are listed – "filial fear, law, kindred, fame" (line 270) – include the erotic complications of several Shakespearean comedies and tragedies. Love, the youth declares, "sweetens" the bitter "aloes" of life's buffets (lines 272–73). He even has the nerve invoke the "bleeding groans" of those who "pine" for him (line 275) as evidence of love's unsubduable power.

As his final tactic of seduction, the youth tells her that all those whom he has hurt "their sighs to you extend / To leave the batt'ry that you make 'gainst mine" heart (lines 276–77), as if she were besieging him rather than the other way around. His final spoken word is "troth," uttered with the "wat'ry eyes" of hypocrisy (lines 280–81). The maiden then tells the old man just how powerfully his tears had moved her:

> O father, what a hell of witchcraft lies
> In the small orb of one particular tear!
> But with the inundation of the eyes
> What rocky heart to water will not wear?
> What breast so cold that is not warmèd here?
>
> (lines 288–92)

Again, lies are seen as the crucial register of the relationship. Rather than the purportedly comfortable mutual lies that imbue the relationship exhibited in Sonnet 138, though, here they are tied to the dark magic of witchcraft and the terrible suffering of hell. Stony self-control is worn down, and cold reason is kindled by passion. She describes in detail the processes by which she succumbed to him:

> For, lo, his passion, but an art of craft,
> Even there resolved my reason into tears;
> There my white stole of chastity I daff'd,
> Shook off my sober guards and civil fears;
> Appear to him, as he to me appears,
> All melting; though our drops this difference bore,
> His poison'd me, and mine did him restore.
>
> (lines 295–301)

Her reason dissolves into tears prompted by his false tears; Shakespeare the actor and playwright knows something about the affective and mimetic power of staged passion. Her resistance melts into the desire he stirs. Chastity is envisioned as an item of clothing that she doffs as easily as she shirks her "sober guards and civil fears" (line 298). In the last line, the tears of both mingle, and become the liquids of sexual passion that are shared in the moment of intercourse. But instead of a pleasurable mutuality, the positive aspects of the intercourse go in only one direction: "His poison'd me, and mine did him restore" (line 301).

A master of the affective conventions of love poetry, the youth calls upon the matter "Of burning blushes, or of weeping water, / Or sounding paleness" in his closing statement (lines 304–05). He is, finally, a master of hypocrisy, using his own staged emotions like an actor to manipulate the emotions of others:

> "Against the thing he sought he would exclaim;
> When he most burn'd in heart-wish'd luxury,
> He preach'd pure maid, and praised cold chastity.
>
> "Thus merely with the garment of a Grace
> The naked and concealed fiend he cover'd."
>
> (lines 313–17)

She absolves herself slightly by calling herself "th' unexperient" (line 318), one whose inexperience keeps her from seeing through such hypocrisy. Like Lucrece, the young woman is made more vulnerable by her very innocence. "Who, young and simple," she asks, "would not so be lovered" (line 320); that is, be possessed by such a lover? She knows that the answer in her case is obvious: "Ay me, I fell" (line 321). The intense focus on her grieving self is underscored by the fact that the line starts with three different sounds that can designate the grammatical first person.

At the end of the poem, the maid wonders "What I should do again for such a sake" (line 322). As she considers this question in the final stanza, she remembers his false emotions with genuine indignation, but the powerful memory of the courtship leads perhaps to a surprising answer:

> O, that infected moisture of his eye,
> O, that false fire which in his cheek so glow'd,
> O, that forced thunder from his heart did fly,
> O, that sad breath his spongy lungs bestow'd,
> O, all that borrow'd motion seeming owed,
> Would yet again betray the fore-betray'd,
> And new pervert a reconciled maid!
>
> (lines 323–29)

If memory was encouraged as a way to preserve the Young Man's beauty in the Sonnets, it is what haunts the woman in *A Lover's Complaint*. The speaker in the Young Man and the Dark Lady sonnets continues to love although he knows the object is untrue, just as the maid in *A Lover's Complaint* continues to feel the pull of a range of seductions she knows are false. Trapped in a cycle of repentance and remembrance, the maid feels the seductive pull of behaviors she would like to shun. Even her confession only provides further occasion for stirring her desire. The poem is in part a study in the compelling power of staged emotion, and of the recursive structures of memory. It is certainly significant that the poem never returns to the narrative voice at the beginning, because that framing would make it possible to distance ourselves from the erotic compulsions of the maid. Ending with her surprising acknowledgment that she would do it all again, the poem, by failing to contain its own narrative, enacts the very process it describes.

"The Phoenix and Turtle"

It is hard to imagine two poems by the same poet that are more different than *A Lover's Complaint* and "The Phoenix and Turtle." If the style of the one is lavish embellishment, the other is spare and cryptic. If the one is a deeply cynical account of both courtship and the ability to control erotic desire, the other is an enigmatic but idealized portrait of the mystical unities of two beings through love. If the one suggests that humans prey on each other like animals in their wish to satisfy sexual desire, the other uses animals to offer a stunning tribute to the physical and spiritual integration of male and female in heterosexual love. Both poems, though, are interested in cycles. Whereas *A Lover's Complaint* explores the pernicious cycles of denial and desire in which the maiden is trapped, "The Phoenix and Turtle" evokes the enigmatic if ultimately liberating cycles of death and rebirth.

We know that "The Phoenix and Turtle" was published in 1601, eight years before *A Lover's Complaint*, in a group of poems by various authors including Ben Jonson that were appended to Robert Chester's *Love's Martyr*. Shakespeare's poem was published without a title, but we will follow tradition in calling it "The Phoenix and Turtle."[4] Assuming that Shakespeare assented to the publication, "The Phoenix and Turtle" is the first poem that Shakespeare had agreed to publish since *Lucrece* in 1594. Chester's poem was printed by Richard Field, who had printed *Venus and Adonis* and *Lucrece*. The full title of Chester's poem gives some sense of its arcane aspirations: "LOVES MARTYR: OR, ROSALINS COMPLAINT. Allegorically shadowing the truth of Love, in the constant Fate of the Phoenix and the Turtle." The phoenix is a mythological creature that periodically consumes itself in fire; from its ashes the phoenix is reborn. The turtle, or turtledove, is a symbol of constancy, and is typically female. The phoenix had long been associated with love poetry, and in 1593 graced the title of one of the most important poetry anthologies of the Elizabethan era: *The Phoenix Nest*, which was compiled and published by a still-unknown "R. S." Chester's poem is long, uninspired, and uninspiring; with numerous digressions, it tells the story of the phoenix, who, on finding the uncharacteristically male turtledove mourning for the loss of its mate, joins with the turtledove in an act of mutual immolation. The poem concludes by predicting that progeny will issue from the couple.

Chester's title solicits an allegorical reading, and subsequent readers have been more than happy to comply.[5] While this may work for Chester's poem, it seems particularly unsatisfying for Shakespeare's, which is concerned with characterizing the mysteries of love and eternity, not allegorizing the details of a particular relationship. Both Chester and Shakespeare likely have Chaucer's *Parlement of Foules* in the back of their minds as they are writing.[6] Written in the rhyme royal stanzaic form Shakespeare used in *Lucrece* and *A Lover's Complaint*, *Parlement* is a dream-vision that portrays a meeting of birds who debate the issue of who should be their mates. Like *Love's Martyr*, the poem seems like it must be about something more than just birds, although critics are not sure what this is. John Skelton's *Philip Sparrow*, the lament of a schoolgirl for her dead bird, may also be a relevant prototype for a poem lamenting the death of a bird. As with the lustful horses in *Venus and Adonis* and the predatory wolf in *Lucrece*, Shakespeare is using the animal kingdom to emblematize human behavior.

In many ways, Shakespeare's poem picks up where Chester's piece ends. Perhaps this is why reading the poem feels as if we have stumbled onto a ritual to which we are not fully privy. The opening line of the poem gestures to a knowledge that we should possess, but do not: "Let the bird of loudest lay." The next line may help a bit, but it also presumes a knowledge of the nesting habits of mythological creatures that is likely not at our fingertips: "On the sole Arabian tree" may designate the Phoenix, since as Sebastian in *The Tempest* cynically remarks after one of Prospero's dumb shows, "Now I will believe . . . that in Arabia / There is one tree the phoenix' throne" (*The Tempest*, 3.3.21–23). But if so, it means that the phoenix is being summoned to deliver its own funeral rites. The whole poem feels as if it were written in a kind of shorthand for which we do not have the key. The style is the polar opposite of the ornate decoration and rhetorical flourish marking all of Shakespeare's other non-dramatic works. In "The Phoenix and Turtle," the chosen medium is aesthetic economy. This spare style gives the poem an incantatory, even oracular, feel. It is something like the Delphic voice of Hymen in *As You Like It*, or the incantatory verse of *Macbeth*. The form of the poem is unique in Shakespeare's non-dramatic corpus; it is a 67-line poem composed of 17 stanzas. Formally, the poem is divided into two sections: the first consists of 13 four-line stanzas, while the second, termed the threnos, consists of 5 three-line stanzas. The first section, moreover, can be subdivided at line 21, as the "anthem doth commence." It is appropriate that a poem focused on the mysteries of unity amid multiplicity would be so aware of its own formal blend of unity and division. The poem repeatedly uses the syntactic structures of logic even as the vocabulary tends to mysticism. This produces a kind of deliberate cognitive dissonance in a reader, as luminous reason and recondite spirituality jostle one another.

It is unclear just what happens in the poem; we do not know whether the consummation is spiritual and/or physical. We also do not know whether a new creature is born from the ashes of their death. At the end of the poem, Shakespeare kills two birds with one flame. In this, his poem resembles Chester's. Both poems, that is, end with the immolation of the "two dead birds." The flames of passion that course through the Sonnets are now becoming something more sublime, but not completely different. The poem seems in part to offer a tribute to the physical and spiritual integration of male and female in heterosexual love. The relationship in "The Phoenix and Turtle," though, produces "no posterity," which contrasts with the emphasis on the progeny produced by heterosexual coupling in the early Sonnets. It is as if the avian protagonists provide Shakespeare with a kind of distance on the idea of love. Love is in this poem valued in and of itself, not for its ability to produce progeny nor for its participation in a usury-based economy. Indeed, in this poem, love is seen to transcend the very mathematics that supplies the fundamental tools of accounting in such an economy: "Number there in love was slain" (line 28).

The poem, then, opens with an imperative:

> Let the bird of loudest lay,
> On the sole Arabian tree,
> Herald sad and trumpet be,
> To whose sound chaste wings obey.
>
> (lines 1–4)

The bird whose identity is in dispute is invited to serve as a herald. The "chaste wings" of the birds may seem like an extraneous detail, but chastity will become a central issue over the course of the poem. The mode of the poem, though, shifts quickly from invitation to prohibition, as the poem excludes a range of birds deemed inappropriate for this occasion:

> But thou shrieking harbinger,
> Foul precurrer of the fiend,
> Augur of the fever's end,
> To this troop come thou not near.
>
> From this session interdict
> Every fowl of tyrant wing,
> Save the eagle, feather'd king:
> Keep the obsequy so strict.
>
> (lines 5–12)

We are not sure what the "shrieking harbinger" (line 5) is, although most commentators have assumed it is the owl, excluded for its proverbial associations with death and the devil as well as its distinctly unmusical song. The poem also endorses a curious political structure in the creatures it invites and excludes – no tyrannical creatures will be allowed to participate, but the monarchical eagle is welcomed. In this detail, the poem seems to glance at England's own necessary fiction of its political structure as a constitutional monarchy that Parliament prevents from degenerating into tyranny.

The poem then offers another round of imperatives, as the various roles in the obsequies, or funeral rites, are cast:

> Let the priest in surplice white,
> That defunctive music can,
> Be the death-divining swan,
> Lest the requiem lack his right.
>
> And thou treble-dated crow,
> That thy sable gender makest
> With the breath thou givest and takest,
> 'Mongst our mourners shalt thou go.
>
> (lines 13–20)

A study in white and black, the swan and the crow have significant roles to play. The swan will be the priest while the crow will be among the mourners. Shakespeare here emphasizes a legend about how crows were thought to propagate not through copulation, but rather by exchanging breath. Like the "chaste wings" in the first stanza, the crow's reproduction via inspiration challenges common models of procreation.

The poem then begins a section it terms "the anthem," and only here do we begin to understand the precise occasion for the obsequies being celebrated:

> Love and constancy is dead;
> Phoenix and the turtle fled
> In a mutual flame from hence.
>
> (lines 22–24)

The "mutual flame" invokes both the passionate love that the two creatures had for each other and the pyre on which they choose to be immolated. Death is imagined as a kind of escape, although we are not sure from what. There is the sense, moreover, that these two birds come to stand for the larger union of love and constancy, something that Shakespeare had sought throughout the Sonnets.

At this point in the poem, the occult language begins to pile up in the effort to convey how the love these two discrete creatures shared produced a mysterious unity:

> So they loved, as love in twain
> Had the essence but in one;
> Two distincts, division none:
> Number there in love was slain.
>
> Hearts remote, yet not asunder;
> Distance, and no space was seen
> 'Twixt the turtle and his queen:
> But in them it were a wonder.
>
> (lines 25–32)

The poem turns to paradox in the effort to describe the mysterious union of two beings in love. In language that begins to adumbrate the mysterious one-ness of the three entities in the Christian Trinity, the poem argues that the two birds are distinct yet undivided. The very processes of rational mathematics are defeated by these creatures for which neither one nor two serves as a sufficient description. We are left only with a sense of "wonder" at the way their desire for each other closes the distance between discrete entities, and challenges the principles of simple addition.

The lovers indeed experience a sense of mutual possession that defies conventional definitions of property and identity:

> So between them love did shine,
> That the turtle saw his right
> Flaming in the phoenix' sight;
> Either was the other's mine.
>
> Property was thus appalled,
> That the self was not the same;

Single nature's double name
Neither two nor one was called.
                    (lines 33–40)

Conventional nomenclature pales beside the beautiful enigma of the avian couple. They truly are "Co-supremes and stars of love" (line 51). Moreover, in a world in which the wife was viewed as the property of her husband, this poem aspires to articulate a remarkable degree of sexual equality, whereby each party is imagined as the mutual possession of the other. It is as if the mystical forces of love are inadequately represented by the terrestrial institutions of legal ownership. Even higher reason is befuddled when it attempts to apprehend the mystery of this love:

> Reason, in itself confounded,
> Saw division grow together,
> To themselves yet either neither,
> Simple were so well compounded,
>
> That it cried, How true a twain
> Seemeth this concordant one:
> Love hath reason, reason none,
> If what parts can so remain.
>
> Whereupon it made this threne
> To the phoenix and the dove,
> Co-supremes and stars of love,
> As chorus to their tragic scene.
>   (lines 41–52)

The "it" that speaks these lines, and the subsequent threnody, is presumably "Reason." Opposites such as "simple" and "compound," "one" and "twain," "love" and "reason," are brought into juxtaposition, perhaps to represent the union of opposites in heterosexual love. What emerges is the portrait of a love that defies conventional definitions of gender, number, property, distance, reason, and identity. Shakespeare, then, turns to the *via negativa*, the definition of something by what it is not that is used most frequently to depict religious mysteries, to describe the devout love of these two creatures. What emerges is a love ultimately defined by its ability to transcend the material circumstances of existence and desire. If most of Shakespeare's non-dramatic works explore the ways that the demands of bodies invariably muddy the phenomenon of desire that they produce, "The Phoenix and Turtle" aspires to articulate a kind of love that fully transcends the physical.

The threnody, or lamentation, that is uttered by Reason has a different form, as if the mysterious union of two in one were being enacted in a single poem composed of two distinct parts. The triplets may also gesture toward some mystical trinity:

> Beauty, truth, and rarity,
> Grace in all simplicity,
> Here enclosed, in cinders lie.
>
> Death is now the phoenix' nest
> And the turtle's loyal breast
> To eternity doth rest,
>
> Leaving no posterity:
> 'Twas not their infirmity,
> It was married chastity.
>
> Truth may seem, but cannot be:
> Beauty brag, but 'tis not she;
> Truth and beauty buried be.
>
> To this urn let those repair
> That are either true or fair
> For these dead birds sigh a prayer.
>
> (lines 53–67)

As is appropriate for this "tragic scene," the poem assumes a lugubrious tone. The death of these two birds occasions the commemoration of a variety of ideals that they symbolized: beauty, truth, rarity, grace, and, as we learned above, love and constancy as well. The various juxtapositions of contradictory terms seem to come to a head in the phrase "married chastity" (line 61). This phrase could mean a marriage in which the virginity of the partners is sustained, or it could mean the kind of profound commitment to absolute fidelity in a deeply physical relationship articulated in Edmund Spenser's *Prothalamion*: "And let your bed with pleasures chaste abound, / That fruitfull issue may to you afford."[7] Shakespeare's poem, though, resists aggressively the long-term consolations of progeny or the short-term comforts of sexuality. The poem concludes with a final invitation that echoes those gestures of welcome at the beginning: those who are either true or fair are invited to come to the urn that holds the ashes of these two marvelous creatures, and to offer a "prayer" for the lovers. The note of devotion that imbues the poem is fulfilled in the concluding invocation to prayer.

There is a sense in which the poem itself is a kind of "well-wrought urn" (to borrow a phrase from Donne's "The Canonization"), the container of the remains of the lovers. Indeed, Donne's remarkable poem shares many features with Shakespeare's.[8] Perhaps most significantly, "The Canonization" exhibits a similar use of the images of birds and the phoenix to represent the mystical union of two lovers:

> And we in us find the eagle and the dove.
>   The Phoenix riddle hath more wit
>   By us; we two being one are it.
> So, to one neutral thing both sexes fit.
> We die and rise the same, and prove
> Mysterious by this love.   (lines 22–27)

Both poems imagine the ultimate internment of the lovers' ashes. But where Donne is seeking approval from a skeptical world for lovers who are passionately alive, Shakespeare's lovers are, it seems, dead beyond any hope of resurrection. In the Sonnets, Shakespeare had imagined that "Devouring Time" (Sonnet 19, line 1) would devastate even the self-regenerating phoenix; time's consummate triumph would be to "burn the long-lived phoenix in her blood" (Sonnet 19, line 4). In "The Phoenix and Turtle," Shakespeare must work hard to make us feel that the phoenix, a figure proverbial for resurrection, is not reborn at the end of the poem. It is as if this poem, like the Sonnets, deliberately avoids such easy answers and facile notions of rebirth, searching instead for the esoteric values that might remain after such an unequivocal and unavoidable death.

Appreciation for this remarkable poem was relatively slow in coming, but it is now safely ensconced as one of the aesthetic pinnacles of Shakespeare's career. John Middleton Murray called it "the most perfect short poem in any language."[9] It may not be Shakespeare's final statement on love, but it is perhaps his most transcendent account of its splendidly esoteric propositions. The poem seems to belie its own claim that "Truth and beauty buried be" (line 61), since its strange, ineffable beauty is so completely wedded to its own aspirations to convey the abstruse truths of love. A poem designed to produce the illusion of hidden meanings that we will never quite fathom, "The Phoenix and Turtle" shadows an ideal love beyond death and reason. Shakespeare imagines that the mutual love the poem describes is a "wonder" that belies terrestrial constructions of human relationships; it is a miracle of sorts, although tragically subject to mortality. The poem's clipped syntax and enigmatic language convey brilliantly the rarity, and the contingency, of such a relationship. It is as if, for Shakespeare, a truly mutual love relationship between two beings is the most amazing miracle of all.

Chapter 8

Fantasies of Shakespearean authorship

Dear son of memory, great heir of fame,
What need'st thou such weak witness of thy name?

– John Milton

One of the great mysteries of English literary history is not "who wrote Shake-speare" but rather "why does the question continue to be asked so frequently, and fervently?" There are probably more conspiracy theories attached to the works historically identified with Shakespeare than to any other body of work in the English literary canon. It is easy for early modern scholars to get cranky about these various theories, particularly when so many notions are mired in snobbery or prejudice, and when there is indeed so little to back them up. We should try, though, to see the gamut of theories as a kind of accidental tribute to the miracle of these works. It is as if their authorship were so magical that it could never be explained by the life or experience of any single individual.

Doubts about Shakespeare's authorship emerge rather late, more than 200 years after his death in 1616. They are largely a product of class and educational snobbery, post-Romantic notions of poetic genius, and historical anachronism. Anti-Stratfordians, as those who doubt Shakespeare's authorship of Shake-speare's works are frequently called, are typically skeptical that a kid from the countryside who lacked a university education and an aristocratic upbringing could become England's most celebrated poet.[1] They also assume anachronis-tically that the lack of documentation around Shakespeare compared to the typical manuscripts and annotated library of a post-Romantic writer is a sign of some conspiracy that needs to be addressed. But, in fact, by early modern standards, Shakespeare's life and career is extremely well documented. By the measure of the typical early modern writer, Shakespeare is not mysterious at all. We know more about him than we know about most, in part because of the immense respect in which he was held by fellow writers and actors, and in part because of the various legal transactions and lawsuits in which he was involved. We are lucky to have as many plays and works as we do, since early modern manuscripts and plays are far more likely to disappear than survive. We have testimonies from people who ate and drank with Shakespeare, who acted in his plays, and in whose plays Shakespeare acted. For the first 200 years after the death of Shakespeare, no doubts are expressed about the authorship of his works.

But it is perhaps telling that the first mention of Shakespeare in print is mired in the kinds of snobbery that still can distort our appreciation of his achievement. In 1592, the year before the publication of *Venus and Adonis*, Shakespeare was already well enough known in London to be attacked in print by the playwright Robert Greene:

> there is an upstart Crow, beautified with our feathers, that with his
> Tiger's heart wrapped in a Player's hide, supposes he is as well able to
> bombast out a blank verse as the best of you: and being an absolute
> Johannes factotum, is in his own conceit the only Shake-scene in a
> country. O that I might intreate your rare wits to be imploied in more
> profitable courses: & let those Apes imitate your past excellence, and
> neuer more acquaint them with your admired inuentions. I know the
> best husband of you all will neuer proue an Usurer, and the kindest of
> them all will neuer seeke you a kind nurse: yet whilest you may, seeke
> you better Maisters; for it is pittie men of such rare wits, should be
> subiect to the pleasure of such rude groomes.[2]

Greene accuses Shakespeare of reaching above his rank by entering a world dominated by such university-educated wits as Greene himself. In case the sneering reference to "Shake-scene" was not sufficient to identify Shakespeare the budding dramatist as the target of Greene's satire, the passage parodies a line from Shakespeare's popular history play, *Henry VI, Part 3* – "Oh, tiger's heart wrapped in a woman's hide." Greene is upset that a "rude groom" would dare to compete with "men of such rare wits."

Shakespeare receives a far more gracious contemporary tribute from Francis Meres, a clergyman, who in 1598 sees Shakespeare as incarnating in his poems and plays English versions of the best of the classical authors:

> As the soul of Euphorbus was thought to live in Pythagoras, so the
> sweet, witty soul of Ovid lives in mellifluous & honey-tongued
> Shakespeare, witness his Venus and Adonis, his Lucrece, his sugred
> sonnets among his private friends, &c.

> As Plautus and Seneca are accounted the best for comedy and tragedy among the Latins, so Shakespeare among the English is the most excellent in both kinds for the stage . . . As Epius Stolo said that the muses would speak with Plautus' tongue if they would speak Latin, so I say that the muses would speak with Shakespeare's fine-filed phrase, if they would speak English.[3]

Meres acknowledges Shakespeare as both a poet and a playwright, the inheritor of the essence of Ovid and Seneca. While *Venus and Adonis* and *Lucrece* had already gone through several editions, the Sonnets were eleven years away from publication, so their mention by Meres is important, as it suggests that Shakespeare likely participated in the process of "manuscript publication" amid a coterie practiced by many early modern authors.[4]

The Passionate Pilgrim

Even if the fantasy that someone else composed the works of Shakespeare emerges very late in reception history, the fantasy of finding a new poem by Shakespeare begins very early. Indeed, its first manifestation is in a collection published in 1599 entitled *The Passionate Pilgrim*. The volume contains twenty poems, only five of which are definitively by Shakespeare. Three of the poems are lyrics from Shakespeare's early comedy *Love's Labour's Lost*, and the other two are sonnets that appear in different versions in the 1609 Quarto. Critics have often assumed that because these poems were published well before the 1609 collection, these are two of the "sugred Sonnets" that Meres describes circulating "among his private friends." While neither of the two poems is particularly *sweet*, they may well have been acquired by the printer, William Jaggard, from a private manuscript.

Several of the poems in *The Passionate Pilgrim* exploit the theme of *Venus and Adonis*, attempting to capitalize on that poem's success as well as its reputation for salacious content. The year 1598 had seen the first appearance of Shakespeare's name on the title page of a printed play, on the quarto publication of *Love's Labour's Lost*, suggesting that "Shakespeare" was becoming a marketable name.[5] *The Passionate Pilgrim* was a success, and in 1612 the third edition of *The Passionate Pilgrim* appeared, printed by William Jaggard, with an expanded title that now emphasized "Certaine Amorous Sonnets, \ betweene Venus and Adonis, | newly corrected and aug- \ mented. | By W. Shakespere." But Jaggard also added several poems by Thomas Heywood that he trumpeted on the title page, including two love epistles Heywood translated from Ovid's *Heroides* which Jaggard had already printed in Heywood's *Troia Britannica or Great Britain's Troy* (1609). Heywood complained about Jaggard's unauthorized use of his work in an epistle he appended to his *Apologie for Actors* (1612); in this epistle, Heywood also makes reference to Shakespeare's unhappiness with Jaggard for using his name without authorization.

> hee, to doe himselfe right, hath since published them in his owne name; but as I must acknowledge my lines not worthy his patronage under whom he hath publisht them, so the author, I know, much offended with M. Jaggard (that altogether unknowne to him) presumed to make so bold with his name.

Heywood suggests that Shakespeare may have had a hand in the publication of the 1609 Sonnets "to doe himself right" (the Sonnets appeared three years before the publication of the third edition of *The Passionate Pilgrim*, but ten years after the second edition); Heywood also implies that Shakespeare was offended by Jaggard's unauthorized use of his name. This suggests that Shakespeare is becoming increasingly aware of his name and work as a form of property to be protected. Jaggard responded by issuing a new title page without Shakespeare's name (but still including, perhaps spitefully, the reference to Heywood's epistles). It is sobering, and perhaps reassuring, to realize that the kind of battling over Shakespeare's name and legacy that still occurs in scholarship and public discourse began in Shakespeare's own lifetime. And it is startling to learn that this contention first surfaces not over Shakespeare as the author of plays but rather over Shakespeare as the author of poems.

Fascinatingly, the whole volume of the *Passionate Pilgrim* was thought to be by Shakespeare for the next 220 years. Only in the nineteenth century did painstaking scholarship begin to sort out what might be by Shakespeare, what is definitely by Shakespeare, and what is definitely the product of other writers. The volume is nonetheless significant because it shows us the kind of poems that were affiliated with Shakespeare's name and reputation. All of the poems are about love, and many discuss Venus, or lamenting females. Shakespeare's immensely successful first publication continues to define the kind of poems that he was likely to write. The volume also inaugurates a genre that is still with us today: the claim to have discovered new work by Shakespeare that one is making available to the public for the first time.

Shakespeare's poem "The Phoenix and Turtle" also appears in a collection by several hands – Robert Chester's *Love's Martyr* (1601) – but, unlike *The Passionate Pilgrim*, that volume does not capitalize on Shakespeare's growing reputation. Its initial title page does nothing to advertise that the volume contains a poem by Shakespeare. The volume was printed by Richard Field,

Shakespeare's fellow Stratfordian (who had achieved such success with *Venus and Adonis* and *Lucrece*), and it is unclear why he did not choose to put Shakespeare's name on the title page. Doing so would have announced that the volume contains a remarkable poem by this increasingly famous and marketable poet.

John Benson, editor

It is even more difficult to say why the volume published in 1609, *Shakespeare's Sonnets*, was not more successful, since Shakespeare's name is featured prominently in the title. Perhaps the fashion for sonnet sequences had so completely waned that even Shakespeare's name could not sell such a sequence. While *The Passionate Pilgrim* goes through a third edition by 1612, the Sonnets are not published again until 1640, and then in a posthumous and drastically altered edition. In *Poems: Written by Wil. Shakespeare. Gent.* (1640), John Benson attempted to do for the non-dramatic poetry what John Heming and William Condell had done for the plays in 1623 when they compiled the First Folio: Benson produces a handsome edition of the collected poems "to be serviceable for the continuance of glory to the deserved Author in these Poems." The book opens with engraver William Marshall's portrait of Shakespeare – a reduced version of Martin Droeshout's engraving from the 1623 First Folio of the plays. This is followed by Benson's preface "To the Reader," and commendatory poems by Ben Jonson, John Milton, and others. The edition combined most of Shakespeare's sonnets (numbers 18, 19, 43, 56, 75, and 76 are omitted, for reasons that are unclear), mingled with poems from *The Passionate Pilgrim* (the 1612 edition), plus *A Lover's Complaint*, and "The Phoenix and Turtle." Benson did not include *Venus and Adonis* and *Lucrece*; this may be a result of their great popularity. Because they were still being actively reprinted, the publisher owned the rights to the text. Benson does, however, include many poems not by Shakespeare at all, but by his contemporaries Christopher Marlowe, Ben Jonson, Thomas Heywood, John Fletcher, and Sir Walter Raleigh. Demonstrating the polyglot nature of a book identified as *Poems: Written by Wil. Shakespeare. Gent.*, the volume also includes poems by several "Cavalier" poets whose popularity was on the rise, including Ben Jonson, Francis Beaumont, and Robert Herrick.

Benson is notorious for rearranging the order of the sonnets into groups, which he then presented as complete poems, with invented titles. The first poem he gives, for example, is a composite of Sonnets 67, 68, and 69, and here entitled "The Glory of Beauty." That "poem" is followed by a composite of

Sonnets 60, 63, 64, 65, and 66 under the title "Injurious Time." Sonnets 113, 114, and 115 are likewise grouped together and entitled "Self-flattery of her Beauty." The Sonnets become in his hands seventy-two distinct poems, many of which are composed of multiple sonnets arranged as stanzas. Perhaps he combined poems since the vogue for sonnets had passed, and he wanted the poems to appear less generically out of date. He also changed the pronouns in three of the sonnets written to a man to create the impression that they were written to a woman; the addressee of Sonnet 108, for example, is changed from "sweet boy," to "sweet love." The titles also sometimes work to reorient poems that in 1609 are likely written to a young man; Sonnet 122 is headed "Upon the receipt of a Table Booke from his Mistriss." Yet he also leaves Sonnet 20 in the collection, and unchanged, except that he gives it a title: "The Exchange." This curious compilation became the "definitive" edition of Shakespeare's poetry until the great eighteenth-century editor Edmond Malone in 1780 asserted the superiority of the 1609 edition of the Sonnets.[6] Benson, though, tries to sell the same fantasy of restored textual authority that Malone was later seeking. Benson's preface "To the Reader," that is, promises somewhat disingenuously that he is presenting poems "which in themselves appear of the same purity, the Author then living himself avouched."

It is easy to be critical of Benson, but one must concede that he had a good eye for the thematic connections that course through the Sonnets. Early modern printers and manuscript copyists, moreover, regularly assumed they had the right, even the duty, to "improve" the poems that they were publishing or transcribing. The first significant anthology of English poetry, *Tottel's Miscellany* (1557, with at least nine other editions before the end of the century), had similarly imposed situational titles on poems that did not possess them in manuscript. Tottel, moreover, also felt free to smooth out Sir Thomas Wyatt's deliberately rough meters.[7] Printers such as Tottel and Benson had a product they were trying to sell, and both did a remarkable job of adapting poems from an earlier time for a rapidly changing literary market. By our editorial standards, however, they did a less than impressive job of presenting the author's work in something like its intended state.

Occasional verse

Throughout the seventeenth century there are scattered bits of occasional verse that are attributed to Shakespeare. None has the philosophical depth or the emotional fireworks that we have come to value in Shakespeare, but it would be somewhat surprising if he did not at times put his immense verbal talents to work for less sublime causes. Indeed, the antiquarian John Aubrey remembers of Shakespeare that

> his father was a Butcher, & I have been told heretofore by some of his neighbours, that when he was a boy he exercised his father's Trade, but when he kill'd a Calfe, he would do it in a high style, & make a speech.[8]

The story may be apocryphal – Aubrey is writing in 1681, and the information is second-hand at best, with plenty of time and opportunity for embellishment. But it would indeed be astonishing if Shakespeare did not sometimes use his powerful linguistic abilities and his remarkable sense of humor in less literary pursuits.

In a manuscript at the Shakespeare Birthplace Trust, for example, is a short poem followed by a note: "Shakespeare upon a pair of gloves that master sent to his mistress." The poem is no masterpiece, but it has formal similarities to the stanza of the threnos in "The Phoenix and Turtle," and is perhaps indicative of a culture that valued the wit required to put even trivial matters into verse:

> The gift is small,
> The will is all:
> Alexander Aspinall.

Aspinall was the schoolmaster at Stratford from 1582 to 1624, too late for Shakespeare to have been his pupil, but it is extremely likely that they knew each other in a town the size of Stratford. Indeed, many of the slight occasional poems attributed to Shakespeare have a clear Stratford provenance. Aubrey suggests that Shakespeare extemporaneously composed the following epitaph on a Stratford neighbor who was "A Noted Usurer":

> Ten in the hundred here lieth engraved;
> A hundred to ten his soul is ne'er saved.
> If anyone ask who lieth in this tome,
> O ho! quoth the devil, 'tis my John-a-Combe.

The first two lines pun on the maximum interest of 10 per cent allowed in the period, and reverse those for the odds of salvation for one who charges such a high rate. John Combe actually left five pounds to Shakespeare in his will, so either Combe had a great sense of humor about himself, or he never saw the mocking epitaph.

In 1602 a lawyer named John Manningham recorded in his diary a fascinating episode about Shakespeare and fellow actor Richard Burbage, suggesting that the marriage of wit and sexuality that marks the love poetry may have been the quotidian milieu of the theatrical companies. Manningham writes that while Shakespeare's popular tragedy *Richard III* was being performed, with Burbage in the title role, Shakespeare and Burbage engaged in a kind of love triangle with a fan:

> Upon a time when Burbage played Richard the Third there was a citizen grew so far in liking with him, that before she went from the play she appointed him to come that night unto her by the name of Richard the Third. Shakespeare, overhearing their conclusion, went before, was entertained and at his game ere Burbage came. Then, message being brought that Richard the Third was at the door, Shakespeare caused return to be made that William the Conqueror was before Richard the Third.[9]

The story may be apocryphal, but it does suit a poet who liked to pun on his first name. It also demonstrates the realm of competitive wit and sexuality that Shakespeare and other players were thought to inhabit, a realm which could turn even the succession of English monarchs into a prop in erotic rivalry.

Indeed, in four separate seventeenth-century manuscripts is a similar example of a contest of wit. Even if this particular episode is fabricated, it certainly represents the convivial social milieu in which Shakespeare was thought to move:

> Master Ben Jonson and Master William Shakespeare being merry at a tavern, Master Jonson having begun this for his epitaph:
> Here lies Ben Jonson,
> That was once one,
> he gives it to Master Shakespeare to make up who presently writes:
> Who while he lived was a slow thing,
> And now, being dead, is no thing.[10]

The lightning wit on display in *Venus and Adonis* and in so many of his plays is here imagined to enable Shakespeare to trump a fellow playwright in a drunken prank. Even if apocryphal, both this episode and Manningham's account of Shakespeare's sexual conquest bespeak the recurring fantasy of Shakespeare's remarkable cleverness and ingenuity.

Shakespeare may have composed the motto that accompanied the shield and crest when in 1596 the request for a Shakespeare family coat of arms was renewed. It is fascinating to imagine Shakespeare literally buying into the very hierarchical distinctions that his plays so frequently mock. The heraldic shield included a spear, punning on the last syllable of the family name, and a falcon spreading its wings in a gesture known as shaking. The motto that accompanied the shield proudly declares "Non sanz droict" (not without right), in appropriately medieval French. The double negative somewhat defensively asserts a nervous claim to long-standing aristocratic privilege, perhaps in response to the early attacks on Shakespeare as an "upstart crow."[11] Shakespeare's friend Ben Jonson apparently could not resist the temptation to mock his friend's social ambition. In a play entitled *Every Man Out of his Humour*, performed in 1599, Jonson has a foolish character purchase a coat of arms with the motto: "Not Without Mustard." Amid the various fantasies of Shakespearean authorship that circulate, it is important to remember that Shakespeare's aesthetic successes granted him an impressive level of material comfort. He accrued wealth and bought property throughout his life. The coat of arms is just another sign of an ambitious and upwardly mobile family.

In 1613, only three years before his death, Shakespeare was hired by the earl of Rutland to devise an *impresa*, or motto, for the Accession Day tilt in March 1613. Richard Burbage, Shakespeare's fellow actor, was hired to design and paint the device. Unfortunately, this piece does not survive, but the record does attest to Shakespeare's successful negotiation of the patronage network in an economy of aristocratic self-display. There may well have been many more such commissions for which all records have been lost.

Two epitaphs in St. Bartholomew's church in Shropshire are attributed to "William Shakespeare the late famous Tragedian." At the east end of the Stanley family tomb (a family Shakespeare may have known, since the dedicatee of *Love's Martyr*, the volume in which "The Phoenix and Turtle" appeared, married a Stanley) are the following verses, which express a profound acceptance of death, and a skepticism about the memorial powers of stone, that is not unlike the Sonnets:

> Ask who lies here, but do not weep.
> He is not dead; he doth but sleep.
> This stony register is for his bones;
> His fame is more perpetual than these stones,
> And his own goodness, with himself being gone,
> Shall live when earthly monument is gone.

At the west end of the tomb are verses which bookend the form and concerns of the poem on the east end:

> Not monumental stone preserves our fame,
> Nor sky-aspiring pyramids our name.
> The memory of him for whom this stands
> Shall outlive marble and defacers' hands.
> When all to time's consumption shall be given,
> Stanley for whom this stands shall stand in heaven.

Except for the explicit invocation of heaven in the second poem and the mention of death as a sleep in the first (and the occasion mandates some sort of religious acknowledgment), the poems rehearse some of the central concerns of the Sonnets. They boldly assert on marble that memory will indeed outlive marble, a material which is like all matter subject to "time's consumption."

Several late seventeenth-century sources attribute to Shakespeare the enigmatic epitaph on his gravestone at Holy Trinity Church, Stratford-upon-Avon:

> GOOD FREND FOR JESUS SAKE FORBEARE,
> TO DIGG THE DUST ENCLOASED HEARE:
> BLESTE BE YE MAN YT SPARES THES STONES,
> AND CURST BE HE YT MOVES MY BONES.

We do not know whether or not these lines were actually composed by Shakespeare for his grave. The concern with the integrity of a corpse is perhaps surprising from the writer who in the Sonnets knows that at death we leave "this vile world" to dwell "with vilest worms" (Sonnet 71, line 4), or who in *Hamlet* could dare to imagine "the noble dust of Alexander . . . stopping a bung-hole" (5.1.188–89). We have no reason to doubt that these lines are by Shakespeare, though, other than their quality and content. The nineteenth-century American writer Mark Twain delivers perhaps the best aesthetic judgment on the question of the poem's quality: "He was probably dead when he wrote it."[12]

These are only a few of the more interesting of the various attributions to Shakespeare in the period after his death. As we look to the recurring quest to discover a new poem by Shakespeare, it is important to see just how frequently poems are attributed to Shakespeare in the seventeenth century and after. Because of the increasing commodity value of his name, people have since his death been ascribing to Shakespeare poems of unclear origin. Despite the claims of increasingly sophisticated stylometric analyses and the gut feelings of scholars who have been studying Shakespeare for thirty years or more, there are no completely reliable measurements for what makes an utterance Shakespearean. As James Shapiro wisely notes, "it's surprisingly hard to distinguish Shakespeare on an off day from one of his imitators on a very good one."[13] In a literary marketplace with little sense of authorial property (copyright law is almost a hundred years away) or textual integrity, it was perhaps inevitable that a writer with the growing cachet of Shakespeare would be exploited by those who stood to profit from doing so. It was also inevitable that various local legends would cluster around this figure of growing fame and significance. It is indeed possible that some of the assignations are actually "authentic," but there exists as yet no reliable litmus test for Shakespearean authorship.

Passionate pilgrims: "Shall I die?" and the *Funeral Elegy*

Recently, there have been two "discoveries" of unknown Shakespeare poems that have received an enormous amount of media attention, and a fair amount of scholarly skepticism. In 1985, Gary Taylor, co-editor of the Oxford Shakespeare, announced a newly discovered work of Shakespeare, the poem "Shall I die?" His primary evidence for this attribution was that a seventeenth-century manuscript assigns it to Shakespeare. The poem had previously been noticed by researchers in the Bodleian Library but had generally been treated as yet another work attributed to Shakespeare with little authority. A seventeenth-century manuscript in the Beinecke Library at Yale University contains a transcription of the same poem without attribution. As we have seen, Shakespeare's name was attached frequently, even promiscuously, to a variety of works. Manuscript anthologies for personal use, moreover, were common during the period, and prove for the most part an unreliable source for authorial attribution.

Perhaps the lyric, which begins with a kind of love lament before it becomes an erotic dream, reminded the compiler of certain moments in Shakespeare; as we have seen, since *Venus and Adonis*, the name of Shakespeare had been associated with explicitly erotic poetry. The poem's clipped style, moreover, shares something with "The Phoenix and Turtle." Assertions about authorship should not be determined solely by subjective judgments of literary quality, but the poem has some good moments; I particularly like the beginning of the second stanza, where the internal rhymes articulate the speaker's erotic and poetic compulsions, and explain in skeleton form the plot of most love poetry:

> Yet I must vent my lust
> And explain my inward pain
>   by my love breeding.
> If she smiles, she exiles
> All my moan; if she frown,
>   all my hope's deceiving.
>   (lines 11–16)

The rest of the stanza, though, is more typical, at once over-wrought and under-thought:

> Suspicious doubt, O keep out,
> For thou art my tormentor.
> Fly away, pack away;
> I will love, for hope bids me venture.
>   (lines 17–20)

The overall literary merit of "Shall I die? Shall I fly" will likely continue to be the subject of scholarly debate, as will its attribution, although a temporary consensus seems to be developing against the claims of Shakespeare authorship. The controversy has been bitter at times, but it has had the salutary effect of encouraging critics and the general public to think about Shakespeare as a non-dramatic poet who wrote under very different circumstances of composition from those that obtain today. It has also been a useful reminder that literary canons are always a construction of sorts, and always contingent on partial and evolving knowledge.

A few years after the initial flurry of public attention surrounding "Shall I die? Shall I fly," another possible "new" poem by Shakespeare emerged, the *Funeral Elegy* by W. S. The poem had been published by Thomas Thorpe, the printer of the 1609 Sonnets, in 1612. In 1989, Donald Foster published a book-length study of the poem, using stylometric analyses to suggest that the poem is likely by Shakespeare.[14] In 1995 Foster argued more strenuously that the poem was in fact by Shakespeare. This provoked a strong, largely negative response in the scholarly community, and the general consensus is that the poem is not by him. Even Foster has conceded that the poem is probably not Shakespeare's. The poem is a long (588 lines), pious, even moralistic elegy on a murdered gentleman from Devon, Sir William Peter. It offers characteristically clumsy and clichéd praise of its subject:

> Those noble twins of heaven-infused races,
> Learning and Wit, refined in their kind
> Did jointly both, in their peculiar graces,
> Enrich the curious temple of his mind;
> Indeed a temple, in whose precious white
> Sat Reason by Religion oversway'd,
> Teaching his other senses, with delight,
> How Piety and Zeal should be obey'd –
> Not fruitlessly in prodigal expense
> Wasting his best of time, but so content
> With Reason's golden Mean to make defence
> Against the assault of youth's encouragement.
>
> (lines 55–66)

But praise of the recently dead rarely brings out the best in poets, then or now; it is possible that deep grief overwhelmed the demands of elaborate aesthetics, making overly conventional sentiments seem peculiarly comforting.

The poem, moreover, offers the hint of scandal and shame around the author of the poem. This odd passage has had the unfortunate effect of encouraging enquiring minds to speculate about what it might mean for our sense of Shakespeare's life:

> Though I, rewarded with some sadder taste
> Of knowing shame, by feeling it have prov'd
> My country's thankless misconstruction cast
> Upon my name and credit, both unlov'd
> By some whose fortunes, sunk into the wane
> Of plenty and desert, have strove to win
> Justice by wrong, and sifted to embane
> My reputation with a witless sin.
>
> (lines 137–44)

The labyrinthine syntax that never quite resolves itself grammatically is certainly not what Shakespeare was capable of on even an average day; perhaps that is what the speaker means by what he infelicitously terms his "witless sin." Recently, Brian Vickers has systematically explored the various possibilities of the authorship of the poem, arguing that it is probably by John Ford, a writer who composed many elegies, and who frequently imitated Shakespeare.[15] We should at the very least be excited by the various questions that the topic of attribution has raised, and remain open to more such moments, since they force us to disclose, and then perhaps to challenge, our own hidden prejudices about the name and work of Shakespeare.

At the same time, the questions and fantasies and attributions that circulate about Shakespeare do attest, albeit backhandedly, to the remarkable aesthetic accomplishments of the works that we have. They suggest that these works are so capacious and compelling that no single life story could really be adequate to explain them. We continue to hope that we will find out more about this inevitably mysterious figure, since he is a figure about whom we could never know enough. In 2009, there was a flurry of academic and popular interest in the possibility that a Jacobean portrait in a family collection in Ireland is a painting from life of Shakespeare. An exhibition at the Shakespeare Centre in Stratford-upon-Avon focused on the portrait, with the title *Shakespeare Found*.[16] That title encompasses the central fantasy of popular and scholarly engagement with Shakespeare – that we will find a painting of Shakespeare, or his notes, or another poem, or a lost play, and suddenly we will understand better the miracle of his literary accomplishments. As long as people read Shakespeare and contemporaneous writers, they will continue to weave fantasies about who wrote Shakespeare, and they will continue to "discover" new poems by Shakespeare. We can only hope that they will read the poems that we know are by Shakespeare with the same vigor and intensity that they devote to speculation about the life and works.

I have to admit that, while writing this book, I had my own fantasy of Shakespearean authorship. I would announce to the public the discovery of a "new" Shakespeare poem – it would, though, be one of the poems we already know, either *Venus and Adonis* or *Lucrece* or "The Phoenix and Turtle." Suddenly that poem would get the full attention it deserves and rewards. It would immediately be the object of at least as much media scrutiny as the far-less-deserving "Shall I die?" or the *Funeral Elegy* (whatever one thinks of the claims of Shakespearean authorship), and a new surge of appreciation for Shakespeare's remarkable body of non-dramatic poetry would swell through the English-speaking world. Students of Shakespeare would of course recognize the poems immediately, but the average reader likely would not. Outside of the Sonnets, I would argue, Shakespeare's non-dramatic canon is critically under-appreciated; I hope that this book, one of the first to consider the entire body of non-dramatic verse, will do something to make these poems more popular once again. The non-dramatic poetry is absolutely critical to our sense of Shakespeare's overall accomplishment, but this is not the best reason for reading these poems. These remarkable poems are of immense importance in their own right, and an unmitigated delight to read, once one has gotten the knack. I hope this book has allowed a few more readers to acquire that knack. Once you have it, the poems will be lifelong companions, changing and growing and deepening with you. This book may not help one learn to talk like Shakespeare, in the manner of Chicago's Shakespeare birthday celebration discussed in chapter 1, but it is intended to help one read Shakespeare's poems. If none of the plays had survived, if these poems were all we had, Shakespeare would still be one of the greatest English writers, a poet who disturbed and advanced every genre he deployed, and who helped create the vocabulary and syntax with which we will still talk about love. It is a remarkable gift for which we should continue to be grateful.

And perhaps the best way of expressing that gratitude is to continue to read the poetry. Shakespeare possessed an extraordinary ability to imagine his poems being read in the future – indeed, many of the claims they make are contingent on their continually being read. In Sonnet 81, for example, the speaker promises the Young Man that "You still shall live (such virtue hath my pen) / Where breath most breathes, even in the mouths of men" (lines 13–14). The poet's pen commands immense power, but that power depends on his work being read. These works are an act of faith in the future, and in the possibilities of a future readership. It is our immense responsibility, and our great delight, to continue to justify that faith.

Notes

1 Shakespeare and English poetry

1 Throughout the book, I will call this work by the name under which it was first published – *Lucrece* – rather than the title it is later (1616) given, *The Rape of Lucrece*. To me, the original title has the virtue of emphasizing the compelling character of Lucrece over the terrible crime that is done to her.

2 See Patrick Cheney, *Shakespeare, National Poet-Playwright* (Cambridge University Press, 2004).

3 Indeed, it is only because the extreme moods caused by the humoral fluids can be so funny to watch, particularly when portrayed on the stage, in the "comedy of humors" pioneered by Shakespeare's friend Ben Jonson, that the modern meaning of humor emerges.

4 Arthur Marotti, "'Love Is Not Love': Elizabethan Sonnet Sequences and the Social Order," *English Literary History* (1982): 396–428.

5 All quotations of Sidney's poetry are from *Sir Philip Sidney: The Major Works*, ed. Katherine Duncan-Jones (Oxford University Press, 2002).

6 George Wright, *Shakespeare's Metrical Art* (Berkeley: University of California Press, 1992), p. 82.

7 On the role of pleasure in Donne, see my "Eloquent Blood and Deliberative Bodies: The Physiology of Metaphysical Poetry," in Thomas Healy and Margaret Healy (eds.), *Renaissance Transformations: The Making of English Writing, 1500–1650* (Edinburgh University Press, 2009), pp. 145–60.

2 Shakespeare's banquet of sense: *Venus and Adonis*

1 In *Shakespeare, National Poet-Playwright* (Cambridge University Press, 2004), p. 76, Patrick Cheney provides a useful list of the plays that Shakespeare had written by 1593, the year in which he published *Venus and Adonis*.

2 On Arthur Golding's translation of the *Metamorphoses*, see *Shakespeare's Ovid*, ed. W. H. D. Rouse (New York: Norton, 1966).

3 C. S. Lewis, *English Literature in the Sixteenth Century* (Oxford University Press, 1954), p. 498.

4 *The Return from Parnassus*, Part 1, Act 4, Scene 1, lines 1,189–1,200, in *The Three Parnassus Plays*, ed. J. B. Leishman (London: Nicholson and Watson, 1949).

5 *The Return to Parnassus*, Part 2, Act 1, Scene 2, lines 301–04.

6 Thomas Middleton, *A Mad World, My Masters* 1.2.47–50; in *Selected Plays*, ed. David Frost (Cambridge University Press, 1978).

7 Sir John Davies, *Papers Complaint, compil'd in ruthfull Rimes Against the Paper-spoylers of these Times*, appended to *The Scourge of Folly* (1611), pp. 232–33.

8 Francis Meres, *Palladis Tamia, Wits Treasury* (London, 1598).

3 Constraint and complaint in *Lucrece*

1 As mentioned in the notes to chapter 1, I choose to call this work by the name under which it was first published – *Lucrece* – rather than the title it is later (1616) given, *The Rape of Lucrece*, in order to emphasize the compelling character of Lucrece over the terrible crime that is done to her.

2 Probably the best account of the poem's republicanism, and the place of republicanism in Shakespeare's career, is available in Andrew Hadfield, *Shakespeare and Republicanism* (Cambridge University Press, 2008).

3 John Kerrigan offers an argument for and an anthology of the early modern genre of female complaint in *Motives of Woe: Shakespeare and Female Complaint* (Oxford University Press, 1991).

4 Kerrigan, *Motives of Woe*, p. 82.

5 G. C. Moore Smith, ed., *Gabriel Harvey's Marginalia* (Stratford-upon-Avon: Shakespeare Head Press, 1913), p. 232.

6 On the cultural importance of this recurring plot, see Heather Dubrow, *Shakespeare and Domestic Loss: Forms of Deprivation, Mourning, and Recuperation* (Cambridge University Press, 1999), and Richard Helgerson, *Adulterous Alliances: Home, State and History in Early Modern European Drama and Painting* (University of Chicago Press, 2000). Helgerson sees in this repeated narrative a statement of the burgeoning political importance of the non-aristocratic home.

7 As we will see in chapter 6, Shakespeare will devote an entire sonnet to the concept of disgust about the thermodynamics and ethics of orgasm; see Sonnet 129, "The expense of spirit."

8 *Oxford English Dictionary*, noun 3. 1. See Deborah G. Burks, "'I'll Want My Will Else': *The Changeling* and Women's Complicity with their Rapists," *English Literary History* 62 (1995): 759–79.

9 Philomel takes her revenge by weaving a tapestry that reveals what was done to her, and then feeding her rapist on a dish made of his children. It is a story that haunts Shakespeare's early violent tragedy *Titus Andronicus*.

10 St. Augustine, *The City of God*, trans. John Healey, 2 vols. (London: Dent, 1945), devotes an entire chapter, Book 1, chapter 18, to Lucrece: vol. 1, pp. 22–24.

11 The prince famously asks of an actor who has been brought to tears in playing the role: "What's Hecuba to him or he to Hecuba, / That he should weep for her?" (2.2.536–37).

12 See Hadfield, *Shakespeare and Republicanism*, pp. 17–53, on the possible connection between the government of republican Rome and the murky concept of England's ancient constitution, which was frequently imagined to limit the power of the monarch.

13 Sonnet 94 is discussed in chapter 6.

4 Mysteries of the Sonnets

1 See Katherine Duncan-Jones, *Ungentle Shakespeare: Scenes from His Life* (London: Arden Shakespeare, 2001), on the various legal matters in which Shakespeare was involved. In "Was the 1609 *Shake-speares Sonnets* Really Unauthorized?" *Review of English Studies* 34 (1983): 151–71, Duncan-Jones argues that the sequence was in some form authorized. In *So Long as Men Can Breathe: The Untold Story of Shakespeare's Sonnets* (Cambridge, MA: Da Capo Press, 2009), Clinton Heylin, better known for his work on Bob Dylan, interestingly compares the 1609 Sonnets to the bootleg recordings that circulated around popular performers such as Dylan, terming the 1609 volume a "bookleg."

2 Other candidates include William Shakespeare himself, William Hathaway, and a boy actor named Willie Hughes. Oscar Wilde's suggestion that Mr. W. H. is a boy actor called Willie Hughes is elaborated in *The Portrait of Mr. W. H.* (1889), in *The Artist as Critic: Critical Writings of Oscar Wilde*, ed. Richard Ellman (New York: Random House, 1969), pp. 152–220.

3 This is the argument of Donald Foster, "Mr. W. H., RIP," *Publications of the Modern Language Association* 102 (1987): 42–54.

4 Francis Meres, *Palladis Tamia, Wits Treasury* (London, 1598).

5 A balanced account of these studies is available in the excellent recent edition of *Shakespeare's Poems*, ed. Colin Burrow (Oxford University Press, 2002), pp. 103–08.

6 Some possibilities for the rival poet include Michael Drayton, Samuel Daniel, George Chapman, Edmund Spenser, Ben Jonson, and, perhaps most likely, Christopher Marlowe.

7 Stephen Booth, ed., *Shakespeare's Sonnets* (New Haven, CT: Yale University Press, 1977), p. 548.

8 Giles Fletcher the Elder, *Licia* (London, 1593): "Epistle Dedicatory," A3.

9 William Wordsworth, lines 2–3, "Scorn not the Sonnet," in *William Wordsworth: The Major Works*, ed. Stephen Grill (Oxford: World's Classics, 200), p. 356; Robert Browning, line 40, "House," in *Poems of Robert Browning*, ed. Tim Cook (Ware: Wordsworth Poetry Library, 1994), p. 530.

10 William Wordsworth, Preface to *Lyrical Ballads* (Bristol, 1798).

11 On numerological readings of the Sonnets, see Alastair Fowler, *Triumphal Forms: Structural Patterns in Elizabethan Poetry* (Cambridge University Press, 1970), and Margaret Healy, *Shakespeare, Alchemy and the Creative Imagination: The Sonnets and A Lover's Complaint* (forthcoming, Cambridge University Press).

12 Heather Dubrow, "'Incertainties Now Crown Themselves Assur'd': The Politics of Plotting Shakespeare's Sonnets," in James Schifter, ed., *Shakespeare's Sonnets: Critical Essays* (New York: Garland, 1999), pp. 113–33.

13 *Midsummer Night's Dream*, 5.1.16–17.

14 Candidates for the real Dark Lady include Amelia Lanyer, mistress to the Lord Chamberlain and the author of the *Salve Deus Rex Iudaeorum* (1611), a devout proto-feminist interpretation of the sacrifice of Jesus; Mary Fitton, a woman impregnated by William Herbert; and Jane Davenant, mother of William Davenant, a writer who claimed that he was the illegitimate offspring of Shakespeare.

15 John Kerrigan, *The Sonnets and A Lover's Complaint* (London: Penguin, 1986), p. 12; Brian Vickers, *Shakespeare, "A Lover's Complaint," and John Davies of Hereford* (Cambridge University Press, 2007). Vickers argues that *The Lover's Complaint* is by John Davies of Hereford. MacDonald Jackson has recently restated his view the *Complaint* shares significant vocabulary with *Cymbeline* and the late plays generally; see "*A Lover's Complaint, Cymbeline*, and the Shakespeare Canon: Interpreting Shared Vocabulary," in *Modern Language Review* 103:3 (July, 2008): 621–38.

16 Ben Jonson, *Timber, or Discoveries made upon men and matter*, in *Ben Jonson and the Cavalier Poets*, ed. Hugh Maclean (New York: Norton, 1974), p. 404.

17 See Margreta De Grazia, "The Scandal of Shakespeare's Sonnets," *Shakespeare Survey* 46 (1996): 35–49 on the Benson edition; and on Malone's editing of Shakespeare, see her *Shakespeare Verbatim: The Reproduction of Authenticity and the 1790 Apparatus* (Oxford University Press, 1991).

18 Probably the most powerful and notorious argument for the Sonnets as the place in which literary subjectivity is invented is Joel Fineman, *Shakespeare's Perjured Eye: The Invention of Poetic Subjectivity in the Sonnets* (Berkeley, CA: University of California Press, 1986).

5 Time and mortality in the Sonnets

1 Sir John Hayward, *An ansvver to the first part of a certaine conference, concerning succession, published not long since vnder the name of R. Dolman* (London, 1603), pp. 17–18.

2 It is perhaps worth noting that in the delightful film *Shakespeare in Love* (1998; written by Marc Norman and Tom Stoppard, directed by John Madden), Shakespeare (played by Joseph Fiennes) is represented as composing the poem after meeting a stunningly beautiful woman, Viola de Lesseps (played by Gwyneth Paltrow).

3 Recent statements of the secularity of the poems include Helen Vendler, *The Art of Shakespeare's Sonnets* (Cambridge, MA: Harvard University Press, 1997), p. 25; Katherine Duncan-Jones, ed., *Shakespeare's Sonnets*, Arden, 3rd series (London: Thomas Nelson, 1997); and two essays in my *Blackwell Companion to Shakespeare's Sonnets* (Oxford: Blackwell, 2006): Richard Strier, "The Refusal to be Judged in Petrarch and Shakespeare," p. 85, and Douglas Trevor, "Shakespeare's Love Objects," p. 240.

4 Suggestions for the missing words include "Feeding," "Lord of," and "Spoiled by."

5 This is a concept that fascinated Shakespeare. In *1 Henry IV* (5.4.84–86), Hal completes Hotspur's dying words ("No, Percy, thou art dust / And food for – ") with the phrase "For worms." And in *Hamlet* (4.3.19–24), Hamlet tells those who are seeking Polonius' body that he is "At supper," but "Not where he eats, but where he is eaten. A certain convocation of politic worms are e'en at him. Your worm is your only emperor for diet. We fat all creatures else to fat us, and we fat ourselves for maggots."

6 John Donne, line 14, Holy Sonnet X, in *John Donne: The Complete English Poems*, ed. C. A. Patrides (London: Dent, 1994), p. 345.

7 On Herbert's use of terrestrial imagery and structures, see my *Prayer and Power: George Herbert and Renaissance Courtship* (Chicago, IL: University of Chicago Press, 1991).

6 Friendship and love, darkness and lust: desire in the Sonnets

1 I am thinking here in particular of the brilliant if overstated work by Joel Fineman, *Shakespeare's Perjured Eye: The Invention of Poetic Subjectivity in the Sonnets* (Berkeley, CA: University of California Press, 1986).

2 For a thorough account of the legibility of female pleasure to early modern men and women, see Valerie Traub, *The Renaissance of Lesbianism in Early Modern England* (Cambridge University Press, 2002).

3 See for example Joseph Pequigney, *Such is My Love: A Study of Shakespeare's Sonnets* (University of Chicago Press, 1985); Bruce Smith, *Homosexual Desire in Shakespeare's England* (University of Chicago Press, 1991); Richard Halpern, *Shakespeare's Perfume : Sodomy and Sublimity in the Sonnets, Wilde, Freud, and Lacan* (Philadelphia, PA: University of Pennsylvania Press, 2002); and Paul Hammond, *Figuring Sex between Men from Shakespeare to Rochester* (Oxford: Clarendon Press, 2002).

4 See Stephen Orgel, *Impersonations: The Performance of Gender in Shakespeare's England* (Cambridge University Press, 1996).

5 On Shakespeare and Petrarch, see Heather Dubrow, *Echoes of Desire: English Petrarchism and its Counterdiscourses* (Ithaca, NY: Cornell University Press, 1995); William J. Kennedy, *The Site of Petrarchism: Early Modern National Sentiment in Italy, France, and England* (Baltimore, MD: Johns Hopkins University Press, 2003); and Richard Strier, "The Refusal to be Judged in Petrarch and Shakespeare," in Michael Schoenfeldt (ed.), the *Blackwell Companion to Shakespeare's Sonnets* (Oxford: Blackwell, 2006), pp. 73–89.

6 See Lily B. Campbell, *Shakespeare's Tragic Heroes: Slaves of Passion* (Cambridge University Press, 1930), and my *Bodies and Selves in Early Modern England: Physiology and Inwardness in Spenser, Shakespeare, Herbert, and Milton* (Cambridge University Press, 1999).

7 Edward Herbert writes a "Sonnet of Black Beauty" and "Another Sonnet to Black Itself," for example, and his brother, the devotional poet George Herbert, writes a Latin poem to Francis Bacon in the persona of an Ethiopian woman entitled "Aethiopissa ambit Cestum Diversi coloris Virum."

8 On the complex issue of color and race in Shakespeare, see Kim Hall, *Things of Darkness: Economies of Race and Gender in Early Modern England* (Ithaca, NY: Cornell University Press, 1995); Ania Loomba, *Shakespeare, Race, and Colonialism* (Oxford University Press, 2002); and Mary Floyd-Wilson, *English Ethnicity and Race in Early Modern Drama* (Cambridge University Press, 2003).

9 John Donne, "Farewell to Love," lines 24–25, in *The Songs and Sonets of John Donne*, ed. Theodore Redpath (New York: St. Martin's Press, 1983), p. 148. The idea that orgasm shortens life derives from Aristotle, but Donne is the only writer I know who asserts this particular ratio.

10 In *Bodies and Selves in Early Modern England*, I explore the connections between desire and disease in early modern physiology. The same connection is parsed in terms of contemporary theory in Jonathan Dollimore, *Death, Desire and Loss in Western Culture* (London: Penguin, 1998).

11 Donne, "The Paradox," lines 7–8, in *Songs and Sonets*, p. 158.

12 See Margaret Healey, *Fictions of Disease in Early Modern England* (Houndmills: Palgrave Macmillan, 2002), on the connections between venereal disease and the baths that were thought to cure it.

7 Solitary and mutual flames: *A Lover's Complaint* and "The Phoenix and Turtle"

1 Brian Vickers, *Shakespeare, "A Lover's Complaint," and John Davies of Hereford* (Cambridge University Press, 2007). Vickers argues that *The Lover's Complaint* is by John Davies of Hereford.

2 James Bednarz, "The Passionate Pilgrim and 'The Phoenix and Turtle,'" in Patrick Cheney, ed., *The Cambridge Companion to Shakespeare's Poetry* (Cambridge University Press, 2007), p. 117.

3 This image is somewhat clumsy to modern ears, but, as Burrow points out, Shakespeare uses the word "stuck" in just this way in two other instances: *Measure for Measure* 4.1.58–59, and *Timon of Athens*, 4.3.262–65; see Colin Burrow, ed., *Shakespeare: The Complete Sonnets and Poems* (Oxford University Press, 2002), p. 700.

4 In *The Complete Sonnets and Poems*, pp. 82–83, Burrow discusses the lack of authority for the title, and explains why he chooses to call it by its first line, "Let the bird of loudest lay."

5 The most common suggestions align the phoenix with Queen Elizabeth, and the turtle with the earl of Essex, or with all of Elizabeth's subjects. Patrick Cheney, *Shakespeare, National Poet-Playwright* (Cambridge University Press, 2004), pp. 187–90, has an amusing account of the various suggestions.

6 Shakespeare's relationship with Spenser and Chaucer is delineated by Patrick Cheney in "The Author's Voice in 'The Phoenix and Turtle': Chaucer, Shakespeare, and Spenser," in Curtis Perry and John Watkins, eds., *Shakespeare and the Middle Ages* (Oxford University Press, 2009), pp. 103–25.

7 Edmund Spenser, *Prothalamion*, lines 103–04, in *Spenser's Minor Poems*, ed. Ernest De Selincourt (Oxford: Clarendon Press, 1910), 3 vols., vol. 1, p. 477.

8 "The Canonization," line 33, in *The Songs and Sonets of John Donne*, ed. Theodore Redpath (New York: St. Martin's Press, 1983), pp. 237–38.

9 Quoted in Cheney, *Shakespeare, National Poet-Playwright*, p. 173.

8 Fantasies of Shakespearean authorship

1 Suggestions for the "real" author of Shakespeare's plays include Francis Bacon, Christopher Marlowe, Edward de Vere, the earl of Oxford, and even Queen Elizabeth. The website Shakespeareauthorship.com does a fine job of answering the various issues brought up by the anti-Stratfordians, those who think that William Shakespeare of Stratford-upon-Avon was not the author of the works that have been attributed to Shakespeare.

2 Robert Greene, *Groats-worth of witte, bought with a million of Repentance* (London, 1592), sig. A3^v.

3 Francis Meres, *Palladis Tamia, Wits Treasury* (London, 1598), fols. 281^v–2^r.

4 See Harold Love, *Scribal Publication in Seventeenth-Century England* (Oxford: Clarendon Press, 1993), and Arthur Marotti, *Manuscript, Print, and the English Renaissance Lyric* (Ithaca, NY: Cornell University Press, 1995).

5 In "Print and Manuscript," in Patrick Cheney, ed., *Cambridge Companion to Shakespeare's Poetry* (Cambridge University Press, 2007), Lukas Erne points out that "Shakespeare's earlier playbooks had been published anonymously, but they started being printed with the author's name on the title page in 1598" (p. 57). He draws from this a fascinating conclusion: "All of a sudden, 'Shakespeare' was a name that sold books."

6 On Benson, see Margreta De Grazia, "The Scandal of Shakespeare's Sonnets," *Shakespeare Quarterly* 46 (1996): 35–49; and on Malone, see De Grazia, *Shakespeare Verbatim: The Reproduction of Authenticity and the 1790 Apparatus* (Oxford: Clarendon Press, 1991).

7 See *Tottel's Miscellany, 1557–1587*, ed. Hyder Rollins, 2 vols. (Cambridge, MA: Harvard University Press, 1965), and Paul Marquis, ed., *Richard Tottel's Songes and Sonettes: The Elizabethan Version* (London: Arizona Center for Medieval and Renaissance Studies, 2008).

8 John Aubrey, *Brief Lives*, ed. John Buchanan-Brown (Harmondsworth: Penguin, 2000), p. 289.

9 *Diary of John Manningham, of the Middle Temple, and of Bradbourne, Kent, barrister-at-law, 1602–1603* (Westminster: J. B. Nichols and Sons, 1868).

10 Included in Colin Burrow, ed., *Shakespeare: The Complete Sonnets and Poems* (Oxford University Press, 2002), p. 725.

11 The coat of arms is well discussed by Katherine Duncan-Jones, *Ungentle Shakespeare: Scenes from His Life* (London: Arden Shakespeare, 2001), pp. 92–97.

12 Mark Twain, *Is Shakespeare Dead? From My Autobiography* (New York: Harper's, 1909). I am sorry to report that for all of his folksy and irreverent brilliance, Twain, like so many Americans, was a notorious anti-Stratfordian.

13 James Shapiro, *A Year in the Life of William Shakespeare: 1599* (New York: Harper, 2005), p. 193.

14 Donald Foster, *Elegy by W. S.: A Study in Attribution* (Newark, DE: University of Delaware Press, 1989). Foster used the same tool successfully to identify the anonymous author of the political novel *Primary Colors*.

15 Brian Vickers, *Counterfeiting Shakespeare: Evidence, Authorship and John Ford's "Funerall Elegye"* (Cambridge University Press, 2009).

16 The claims about the painting are discussed with skepticism and intelligence by Katherine Duncan-Jones, "Unfound(ed)? The Real Identity of the Sitter for a 'Shakespeare' Portrait," *Times Literary Supplement*, 20 March 2009, p. 7.

Further reading

Editions of Shakespeare's poems

Some of the finest recent work on Shakespeare's poetry has occurred in the various editions that have been published over the latter part of the twentieth century. Stephen Booth's edition of *Shakespeare's Sonnets* (New Haven, CT: Yale University Press, 1977) is a remarkable and inimitable study in the power of close reading. Other notable editions include John Kerrigan, ed., *"The Sonnets" and "A Lover's Complaint"* (Harmondsworth: Penguin, 1995), which makes a strong case for the authorship and importance of *A Lover's Complaint*; Helen Vendler, *The Art of Shakespeare's Sonnets* (Cambridge, MA: Harvard University Press, 1997), probably the best account we have of the Shakespearean quatrain as a unit of poetic meaning; Colin Burrow, ed., *The Complete Sonnets and Poems* (Oxford University Press, 2002), a wonderfully balanced presentation of all the non-dramatic poems; Barbara A. Mowat and Paul Werstine, eds., *Shakespeare's Sonnets and Poems* (New York: Washington Square Press, 2004); John Roe, ed., *The Poems* (Cambridge University Press, 2006); G. B. Evans, ed., *The Sonnets*, intro. Stephen Orgel (Cambridge University Press, 2006); and Katherine Duncan-Jones and Henry Woudhuysen, eds., *Poems*, Arden 3rd series (London: Thomson Learning, 2006).

Biographies of Shakespeare

Illuminating, readable, and reliable recent biographies of Shakespeare include Samuel Schoenbaum, *William Shakespeare: A Documentary Life* (Oxford University Press, 1975), which reprints all the crucial documents from Shakespeare's life; Richard Dutton, *William Shakespeare: A Literary Life* (Basingstoke: Macmillan, 1988); Russell Fraser, *Young Shakespeare* (New York: Columbia University Press, 1988), and *Shakespeare: The Later Years* (New York: Columbia University Press, 1992); Dennis Kay, *Shakespeare: His Life, Work and Era* (New York: William Morrow, 1992); Stanley Wells, *Shakespeare: The Poet and His Plays* (London: Methuen, 1997); Park Honan, *Shakespeare: A Life* (Oxford University Press, 2000); Katherine Duncan-Jones, *Ungentle Shakespeare: Scenes from His Life* (London: Arden Shakespeare, 2001); Stephen Greenblatt, *Will in the*

World: How Shakespeare Became Shakespeare (New York: Norton, 2004); James Shapiro, *A Year in the Life of William Shakespeare: 1599* (New York: Harper Collins, 2005); and Jonathan Bate, *Soul of the Age: A Biography of the Mind of William Shakespeare* (New York: Random House, 2009).

Works on Shakespeare's poetry

Significant recent books on Shakespeare's poetry include Eckbert Faas, *Shakespeare's Poetics* (Cambridge University Press, 1986); Heather Dubrow, *Captive Victors: Shakespeare's Narrative Poems and the Sonnets* (Ithaca, NY: Cornell University Press, 1987); Dennis Kay, *William Shakespeare: Sonnets and Poems* (New York: Twayne, 1998); Stephen Orgel and Sean Keilen, eds., *Shakespeare's Poems* (New York: Garland, 1999); A. D. Cousins, *Shakespeare's Sonnets and Narrative Poems* (Harlow: Longman, 2000); Peter Hyland, *An Introduction to Shakespeare's Poems* (Basingstoke: Palgrave Macmillan, 2003); Sasha Roberts, *Reading Shakespeare's Poems in Early Modern England* (Basingstoke: Palgrave Macmillan, 2003); Patrick Cheney, *Shakespeare, National Poet-Playwright* (Cambridge University Press, 2004); Patrick Cheney, ed., *The Cambridge Companion to Shakespeare's Poetry* (Cambridge University Press, 2007).

Works on Shakespeare's Sonnets

Helpful books that focus on the Sonnets include Stephen Booth, *An Essay on Shakespeare's Sonnets* (New Haven, CT: Yale University Press, 1972); Gerald Hammond, *The Reader and Shakespeare's Young Man Sonnets* (London: Macmillan, 1981); Joseph Pequigney, *Such Is My Love: A Study of Shakespeare's Sonnets* (University of Chicago Press, 1985); Joel Fineman, *Shakespeare's Perjured Eye: The Invention of Poetic Subjectivity in the Sonnets* (Berkeley, CA: University of California Press, 1986); James Schiffer, ed., *Shakespeare's Sonnets: Critical Essays* (New York: Garland, 1999); David Schalkwyk, *Speech and Performance in Shakespeare's Sonnets and Plays* (Cambridge University Press, 2002); Paul Edmondson and Stanley Wells, *Shakespeare's Sonnets* (Oxford University Press, 2004); Michael Schoenfeldt, ed., *A Companion to Shakespeare's Sonnets* (Oxford: Blackwell, 2006); Dympna Callaghan, *Shakespeare's Sonnets* (Oxford: Blackwell, 2007); Robert Matz, *The World of Shakespeare's Sonnets: An Introduction* (Jefferson, NC: McFarland, 2008).

The interested reader should also consult Heather Dubrow, *Captive Victors: Shakespeare's Narrative Poems and the Sonnets* (Ithaca, NY: Cornell University Press, 1987); Dennis Kay, *William Shakespeare: Sonnets and Poems* (New York: Twayne, 1998); Stephen Orgel and Sean Keilen, eds., *Shakespeare's Poems* (New York: Garland, 1999); A. D. Cousins, *Shakespeare's Sonnets and Narrative Poems*

(Harlow: Longman, 2000); Peter Hyland, *An Introduction to Shakespeare's Poems* (Basingstoke: Palgrave Macmillan, 2003); Sasha Roberts, *Reading Shakespeare's Poems in Early Modern England* (Basingstoke: Palgrave Macmillan, 2003); and Patrick Cheney, *Shakespeare, National Poet-Playwright* (Cambridge University Press, 2004).

Works on *Venus and Adonis*

There are not a lot of individual books on Shakespeare's first and most popular poem, but the reader should consult Philip C. Kolin, ed., *Venus and Adonis: Critical Essays* (New York: Routledge, 1997); Yve Peyre and François Laroque, *William Shakespeare: Venus and Adonis* (Paris: Dider Erudition and CNED, 1998); and Anthony Mortimer, *Variable Passions: A Reading of Shakespeare's "Venus and Adonis"* (New York: AMS Press, 2000). The interested reader should also explore Heather Dubrow, *Captive Victors: Shakespeare's Narrative Poems and the Sonnets* (Ithaca, NY: Cornell University Press, 1987); Jonathan Bate, *Shakespeare and Ovid* (Oxford University Press, 1994); Dennis Kay, *William Shakespeare: Sonnets and Poems* (New York: Twayne, 1998); Stephen Orgel and Sean Keilen, eds., *Shakespeare's Poems* (New York: Garland, 1999); A. D. Cousins, *Shakespeare's Sonnets and Narrative Poems* (Harlow: Longman, 2000); Peter Hyland, *An Introduction to Shakespeare's Poems* (Basingstoke: Palgrave Macmillan, 2003); Sasha Roberts, *Reading Shakespeare's Poems in Early Modern England* (Basingstoke: Palgrave Macmillan, 2003); Patrick Cheney, *Shakespeare, National Poet-Playwright* (Cambridge University Press, 2004); and Coppelia Kahn, *"Venus and Adonis,"* in Patrick Cheney, ed., *The Cambridge Companion to Shakespeare's Poetry* (Cambridge University Press, 2007), pp. 72–89.

Works on *Lucrece*

There are few books dedicated exclusively to Shakespeare's ambitious second published poem, but the reader can consult R. Thomas Simone, *Shakespeare and Lucrece: A Study of the Poem and Its Relation to the Plays* (Institut für Englishe Sprache und Literatur, Universität Salzburg, 1974); Ian Donaldson, *The Rapes of Lucretia: A Myth and Its Transformations* (New York: Oxford University Press, 1982); and Stephanie Jed, *Chaste Thinking: The Rape of Lucretia and the Birth of Humanism* (Bloomington, IN: Indiana University Press, 1989). The interested reader should also consult Heather Dubrow, *Captive Victors: Shakespeare's Narrative Poems and the Sonnets* (Ithaca, NY: Cornell University Press, 1987); Jonathan Bate, *Shakespeare and Ovid* (Oxford University Press, 1994); Dennis Kay, *William Shakespeare: Sonnets and Poems* (New York: Twayne, 1998); Stephen Orgel and Sean Keilen, eds., *Shakespeare's Poems* (New York: Garland, 1999); Heather Dubrow, *Shakespeare and Domestic Loss: Forms of Deprivation,*

Mourning, and Recuperation (Cambridge University Press, 1999); A. D. Cousins, *Shakespeare's Sonnets and Narrative Poems* (Harlow: Longman, 2000); Peter Hyland, *An Introduction to Shakespeare's Poems* (Basingstoke: Palgrave Macmillan, 2003); Sasha Roberts, *Reading Shakespeare's Poems in Early Modern England* (Basingstoke: Palgrave Macmillan, 2003); Patrick Cheney, *Shakespeare, National Poet-Playwright* (Cambridge University Press, 2004); Catherine Belsey, "The Rape of Lucrece," in Patrick Cheney, ed., *The Cambridge Companion to Shakespeare's Poetry* (Cambridge University Press, 2007), pp. 90–107; and Andrew Hadfield, *Shakespeare and Republicanism* (Cambridge University Press, 2008).

Works on *A Lover's Complaint* and "The Phoenix and Turtle"

As one might expect, there are not many books that focus on these two singular poems, but the reader interested in knowing more about "The Phoenix and Turtle" should explore G. Wilson Knight, *The Mutual Flame: On Shakespeare's Sonnets and the Phoenix and the Turtle* (London: Methuen, 1955); William H. Matchett, *"The Phoenix and the Turtle": Shakespeare's Poem and Chester's "Loues Martyr"* (London: Mouton, 1965); Richard Allan Underwood, *Shakespeare's "The Phoenix and Turtle": A Survey of Scholarship* (Institut für Englishe Sprache und Literatur, Universität Salzburg, 1974); Patrick Cheney, *Shakespeare, National Poet-Playwright* (Cambridge University Press, 2004), chapter 6; Lynn Enterline, "'The Phoenix and the Turtle,' Renaissance Elegies, and the Language of Grief," in Patrick Cheney, Andrew Hadfield, and Garrett A. Sullivan, eds., *Early Modern English Poetry: A Critical Companion* (Oxford University Press, 2007), pp. 160–71; James Bednarz, *"The Passionate Pilgrim* and 'The Phoenix and the Turtle,'" in Patrick Cheney, ed., *The Cambridge Companion to Shakespeare's Poetry* (Cambridge University Press, 2007), pp. 108–24; and Patrick Cheney, "The Author's Voice in 'The Phoenix and Turtle': Chaucer, Shakespeare, and Spenser," in Curtis Perry and John Watkins, eds., *Shakespeare and the Middle Ages* (Oxford University Press, 2009), pp. 103–25.

There is a somewhat more extensive critical conversation about *A Lover's Complaint*: John Kerrigan, *Motives of Woe: Shakespeare and "Female Complaint": A Critical Anthology* (Oxford University Press, 1991); Shirley Sharon-Zisser, ed., *Critical Essays on Shakespeare's "A Lover's Complaint": Suffering Ecstasy* (Aldershot: Ashgate, 2006); and Brian Vickers, *Shakespeare, "A Lover's Complaint," and John Davies of Hereford* (Cambridge University Press, 2007). The interested reader should also consult Patrick Cheney, *Shakespeare, National Poet-Playwright* (Cambridge University Press, 2004), chapter 8; Margaret Healy, "'Making the quadrangle round': Alchemy's Protean Forms in Shakespeare's Sonnets and *A Lover's Complaint*," pp. 405–25, and Catherine Bates, "The Enigma of *A Lover's Complaint*," pp. 426–40, both in Michael Schoenfeldt, ed., *A Companion to Shakespeare's Sonnets* (Oxford: Blackwell, 2006); and Katharine

Rowe, "*A Lover's Complaint,*" in Patrick Cheney, ed., *The Cambridge Companion to Shakespeare's Poetry* (Cambridge University Press, 2007), pp. 144–60.

Works on Shakespeare the poet, his reputation, and his influence

All scholars of Shakespeare's poetry are indebted to the monumental accomplishment of Hyder Rollins, ed., *A New Variorum Shakespeare: The Poems* (Philadelphia, PA: Lippincott, 1938), and *A New Variorum Shakespeare: The Sonnets,* 2 vols. (Philadelphia, PA: Lippincott, 1944). The six volumes of Brian Vickers, ed., *Shakespeare: The Critical Heritage* (London: Routledge, 1974–81) contain a wealth of material, as does C. M. Ingleby et al., eds., *The Shakespere Allusion-Book: A Collection of Allusions to Shakespeare from 1591 to 1700,* rev. John Munro, 2 vols. (Freeport, NY: Books for Libraries Press, 1970). A provocative and learned account of the cultural stakes of Shakespeare's reputation is available in Gary Taylor, *Reinventing Shakespeare: A Cultural History from the Restoration to the Present* (Oxford University Press, 1989). In *Shakespeare Only* (University of Chicago Press, 2009), Jeffrey Knapp explores the inherited and unique models of authorship Shakespeare inhabited in the poems as well as the plays. A balanced and readable account of the authorship controversy is available in James Shapiro, *Contested Will: Who Wrote Shakespeare?* (New York: Simon and Schuster, 2010).

Internet resources for studying Shakespeare

These resources grow and change daily, it seems, but a well-annotated and up-to-date guide to Shakespeare on the internet is "Mr. William Shakespeare and the Internet," http://shakespeare.palomar.edu/. Also helpful is the website of the Shakespeare Birthplace Trust http://www.shakespeare.org.uk/. Various editions of Shakespeare's works are available at http://internetshakespeare.uvic.ca/index.html from the University of Victoria; at the Electronic Text Center at the University of Virginia: http://etext.virginia.edu/shakespeare/; and at a site maintained by MIT: http://shakespeare.mit.edu/. Texts of the works of Shakespeare and his contemporaries are also available at Early English Books Online: http://eebo.chadwyck.com/home.

Index

Cambridge Introductions to Literature

AUTHORS

TOPICS

Printed in the United States
By Bookmasters